JOURNEY TOWARD FREEDOM

True Stories of Faith-Based Recovery
In the Pacific Northwest

Freedom House

Published in Beaverton, Oregon, by Good Catch Publishing.
www.goodcatchpublishing.com
V1.1

Printed in the United States of America

Table of Contents

DEDICATION

This book is dedicated to the many men and women who have found freedom through discipleship and the development of strong Christian character. God's word is proven and true.

I also share my heartfelt thanks to those who have stood alongside us, whether it is as sponsoring partners, dedicated staff, selfless volunteers or our family members who have all given sacrificially of themselves to help the broken find hope and healing.

Finally, I thank my Savior who reached into the gutter and pulled me out. He is the one who set me free, won my heart and is worthy of all my praise.

Pastor Jim Cottrell

ACKNOWLEDGEMENTS

I would like to thank Jim Cottrell, Freedom House Ministries Director, for the vision, hard work, prayer and faith he put into this book to make it a reality; and the men at Freedom House for their boldness and vulnerability in telling the stories that comprise this compilation of real life stories.

This book would not have been published without the amazing efforts of our project manager, Marla Lindstrom Benroth. Her untiring resolve pushed this project forward and turned it into a stunning victory. Thank you for your great fortitude and diligence. I would also like to thank our invaluable proofreader, Melody Davis, for all the focus and energy she has put into perfecting our words. Lastly, I want to extend our gratitude to Evan Earwicker, our graphic artist, whose talent and vision continually astounds us. We are so blessed to have you as a part of this team.

Daren Lindley
President and CEO
Good Catch Publishing

The book you are about to read
is a compilation of authentic life stories.
The facts are true, and the events are real.
These storytellers have dealt with crisis, tragedy, abuse and neglect
and have shared their most private moments, mess-ups and
hang-ups in order for others to learn and grow from them.
In order to protect the identities of those involved in their pasts,
the names and details of some of the people mentioned in this
book have been withheld or changed.

INTRODUCTION

The ravages of drug abuse, alcoholism, gambling, pornography and other life-controlling problems damage the lives of those we love and those we know on a daily basis. Secular recovery is a multi-billion dollar industry, despite the prevention messages and warnings of every type we hear wherever we turn. Yet, things seem to get worse, not better. Most would agree that the problem is pandemic, and our culture is in crisis.

Is there an answer to the devastating condition on our streets? Do miracles still happen? Walk with us through these pages as we share the true stories of men who found freedom through faith-based recovery and discipleship. Together, let's share the good news of hope and a future worth living when we are willing to walk along this *Journey Toward Freedom.*

COMING HOME
The Story of Ryan Smith
Written by Kevin Gill

"Freedom House is no longer an option for you," Jim said. "You've done a great job of fooling everybody, and I think you're trying to fool us again. You've blown every chance everyone has ever given you, and I don't believe there's anything we can do for you."

"I have to come here," I insisted. "If I leave, I'm going to kill myself. I mean it."

"Ryan, you've already proven that you don't want to change. Your coming here would be a waste for both of us. And we need to spend our efforts with the people who truly want to change. Honestly, being here won't do you any good. I mean, look at you — you're even stoned right now!"

As I stared down at the desk, tears fell across my cheeks, and the gravity of my situation finally struck home. I was truly at the end of the line. For me, the streets meant death, plain and simple. Without help, there was no way I could stay clean. And each time I went back to drugs, I couldn't keep myself from using more and more. My mind raced over the hundreds of times I'd made the wrong choice, and as I saw my hope fade away, I couldn't help but think back to exactly how I'd let my life fall so completely apart.

I thought of my family.

***

"All you need to do to go to heaven is ask Jesus into your heart." My mother's voice felt sweet to my 7-year-old ears. I don't know why, but I did want to go to heaven.

I wiped my wavy brown hair from my forehead, clasped my hands together and closed my eyes. "Jesus, please come into my heart. Please come into my heart. Please —" I repeated the same phrase at least 20 times because I wanted to be absolutely sure I got it right.

"I'm so proud of you!" my mother said, sweeping me up in a big hug. Her hair tickled my face, and I squirmed a bit until she put me down. "You're going to heaven!" She planted several kisses on my forehead. "Now, it's time to go back to your lessons."

"No."

My mother's happiness quickly turned into exasperation. "I'm doing this for you! Why won't you just obey me?" my mother yelled.

I looked her straight in the eye. "Because I don't want to."

But no matter how hard I fought, she still managed to get me to study. But once I turned 13 years old, I started to fight a lot harder. I grew more rebellious with each passing day, constantly fighting, constantly pushing my mother's hot buttons. My father always worked during this time, doing his best to provide for us. So the battle of wills was mainly between me and my mother. I'd grown more difficult to deal with. And whenever I could, I worked on my mother's emotions, always looking for the breaking point. My antics wore on her until, finally, I won.

But my victory came at a cost — my mother sent me to public school.

No matter how much I loathed the idea of attending a public school there was no way out. I was going to have to mingle with all the normal kids. That idea both intrigued and scared me. I'd been home schooled my entire life, which had allowed me to avoid the embarrassment of my family's financial difficulties.

We'd managed to move into a four-bedroom house the year before, but prior to that, I'd spent my first 12 years growing up in a singlewide mobile home, tussling for space with my older brother and sister. And now, even though we lived in a normal house, I still harbored doubts about how well I'd be accepted. Money was tight, which meant I wouldn't be dressed in the trendy fashions, but that thought paled in comparison to the knowledge that I'd have to get up early in order to spend the day having strangers tell me what to do.

School turned out to be every bit as dreadful as I thought it would. So when Leo, a new friend from school, came over to our house and pulled out a small marijuana pipe, I was intrigued.

I'd never tried drugs before, but the thought of doing something I wasn't supposed to do was too tempting to pass up. We climbed onto the roof to hide the smoke from my parents. There wasn't much marijuana in the pipe, but we each managed to take one hit before it was gone. But I was high, nonetheless — with the kind of euphoria that comes from living on the edge, doing things my own way.

A couple days later, Leo invited me to go to the mall with his family. He was a bit older than me, and although he didn't participate in any team sports, was quite an athlete. His parents, two hardworking, hard drinking prior divorcees, left us to go wander by ourselves. Neither of us had any cash so we browsed through the stores, picking things up and putting them back down, trying to look like we could afford anything that caught our fancy.

We wandered into the camping section of a sports shop.

"It stinks being poor, not able to buy stuff," Leo complained. He picked up a plastic package. "Wouldn't you like one of these lighters?"

"Sure," I replied, shrugging.

He handed it to me. "All you need to do is pop the back out on one of these plastic packs, then leave the pack and walk away with the lighter. Nobody will know."

Leo watched to see what I would do. I looked back and forth from his curious face to the lighter. I saw a spark of doubt in his eye that lit my desire to prove him wrong.

I casually picked up the pack and popped the lighter out the back, just like Leo had said. Its plastic felt a bit chilly as I wrapped my fingers around it, and I put the lighter pack back on the shelf.

We casually strolled out of the store and walked into a public bathroom. I'd almost expected some sort of commotion, but nobody noticed us. Nothing seemed to change. The earth kept revolving.

Leo tried to snatch the lighter from me. "Dude, I can't believe you actually did it. Give it here!"

"No way," I replied. "It's mine." I held it away from him until he gave up trying to get it. Then, I pulled my thumb across the lighter's serrated roller bringing a spark to gas vapor. The flame was three inches tall, and while Thomas Edison had a light bulb revelation, my revelation was one born of primitive fire.

I wasn't really poor — not if I could simply take the things I wanted. Money wasn't a problem anymore. I could have anything in the world. All I had to do was steal it.

But stealing marijuana was all but impossible. Only users had it, and I didn't want to steal from anybody I knew. So I wondered how I could get some drugs. But Leo had a solution.

"My friend's brother has ADD. You know Adderall? It's like meth in a pill, man. You'll stay awake and feel good for hours. Wanna try?"

"You have some?"

"Yeah, my friend takes them from his brother's prescription. It's no big deal; his brother doesn't take them very much, anyway." He handed me a few pills, and I downed them without a second thought. One hour later, I was already asking him how I could get more.

"Sorry, man, I'm out. My friend can't get any until his brother gets his prescription filled again."

Leo and I, unwilling to accept defeat so easily, set ourselves to brainstorming how to make money for marijuana.

"Dude," I said during a lunch break, "if we ask 10 people for a dollar each, we can score a dime bag of weed."

That's all the inspiration it took. We had to ask way more than 10 people for money, but numbers didn't matter now that we had our goal within striking distance. By the end of the school day, we pooled our take and had exactly 10 bucks. We were officially beggar-entrepreneurs — also referred to as "budding dope fiends."

One day at lunch in the cafeteria, we ended up sitting next to another drug user who attended our school, Mark.

Mark looked giddy. He kept running his fingers through his stringy brown hair and was acting like everything in the world was a new experience. His cloudy eyes alternately darted randomly, then stared at something as though it was absolutely captivating.

"What's going on?" I asked.

"Nothing," he replied quickly. But he started to chuckle under my continued scrutiny and let loose his secret. "I found out about something. Coricidin. Seriously. They're this over-the-counter medication. But you take like 10 of them and *wow*. I mean it. Like — *wow!*"

He looked like he was having so much fun that I grew jealous.

"You want to try some?" he asked. "I've got like 20 more."

It didn't take more than a second for me to decide.

"Yeah, man."

We reconvened in the boys' bathroom and waited for everyone else to clear out. Once we were alone, Mark poured some pills into his hand from an aspirin bottle and meticulously counted them out. He handed me exactly 10.

COMING HOME

They tasted like candy and were easy to swallow. The effects started to hit in 10 minutes. Within 20 minutes, it was like all my cares had dissolved into euphoria.

The Coricidin soared through me, and I felt like I was floating in a dozen directions at once. I'd found my drug of choice. It got me high, and because it was available over the counter, it would always be easy to get more. All I'd have to do is steal it. No more begging for money, no more waiting for a prescription to be filled. I could have as many as I wanted, as often as I wanted — I was in my version of the promised land.

***

Coricidin spread through the high school like wildfire. Virtually everybody I hung out with tried it, loved it and became a habitual user. It was legal, and its effects faded away in a somewhat enjoyable manner. It didn't leave me sick or drowsy; it had more of an afterglow effect, like a runner after a competition. Tired, elated and already planning to run the next race.

Lori, Mark's girlfriend, had a car so she became our "go-to" person. Every day after school, the three of us headed to a different store. We'd browse around as if we were shopping, then when nobody was paying attention to us, one or two of us would grab several bottles of Coricidin and take them into the bathroom. Then, we'd open them and transfer all the pills into plastic bottles we'd smuggled in.

I gave these pills to my closest friends or sold them to anyone who had money. I finally had both drugs and money, and I couldn't imagine how things could be better.

Several weeks later, after a theft run, I headed over to Leo's house to give him 20 pills. He opened the door, and we walked into his living room. His parents were both working, leaving us plenty of freedom to get stoned at his house.

Leo took 10 pills and flipped on the television. He scanned the channels, finally stopping on the evening news.

A middle-aged male reporter spoke:

"In other news, there's a new rash of drug use spreading through the high schools of America. Coricidin, an over-the-counter cough medication, has become the drug of choice for thousands of teenagers across the country. It's also known as

21

'Triple C' and 'Skittles' due to its candy coating that makes it particularly appealing to youth. Over to you, Linda."

"The primary danger comes from its inactive ingredient, meant to treat high blood pressure. In high doses, its effect actually reverses causing the heart rate to rise, leading to heart palpitations, seizures, heart attacks and even death. So far, the death count has reached more than 40 students. Here's what some of our nation's high schoolers are saying —"

The reporter interviewed several teenagers about whether they knew anybody who used Coricidin. Yes, they all knew somebody who took it. No, they would *never* take it themselves (I was sure some of them were lying). Yes, they knew it was extremely dangerous (lying again), and yes, they thought it was important for students to help police their friends.

Leo's phone rang. Without thinking, I picked it up.

"It's Ryan."

"Ryan, it's Lori," she sobbed. "Mark overdosed, and he's in the hospital."

"Is he okay?"

"I don't know. I don't know. Oh, God. You've got to stop taking that, Ryan. I mean, you've been using even more than Mark, haven't you?"

"Don't worry, I'll stop."

A couple of the other users called us that night, as well. They were adamant. "We have to stop taking that stuff. We're done. You're done, too, right?"

I agreed with them and promised I was finished.

***

Everyone *did* stop taking it — except me. I backed off for a couple days, but it wasn't long before I was back up to 20 pills, 30 pills ... *I can't overdose,* I thought. *That kind of thing only happens to other people from other schools. Mark just had a freak accident.*

The news of Mark's overdose passed from parent to parent until everyone associated with our school had heard about it. The next morning, I took 60 pills before heading downstairs to float my way to school. My father stopped me.

"Ryan, I know about your friend Mark. You hang out with him a lot, right? You're not taking any pills or anything. I mean, Coricidin or anything else like that, are you?"

"No, Dad," I lied quickly. Lying about it felt as natural as saying, "Here's your morning paper," or "I'm back home."

"I'm really glad. That stuff is dangerous. All drugs are very dangerous."

I literally floated to school. I didn't move, the world moved around me. The first two periods passed like time formed a wormhole and sucked me through.

Then came gym class.

"Form up!" yelled the chubby gym teacher. "Volleyball!"

Lori approached me as we stood on the court, waiting to return the other team's serve.

"Someone lit a fire in the bathroom earlier," she whispered. "Was it you?"

I shook my head. I hadn't done it, but I could understand why someone might assume I did. I always had a lighter and a reputation for being up to what most people labeled as "no good."

"Zero serving zero," a girl's voice echoed across the shiny gymnasium floor. A moment later, there was a dull thump as she struck the volleyball and sent it arcing high over the net.

As our teams volleyed back and forth, my heart picked up speed. The ball arced toward me. I sent it back over the net. I felt my chest pound a bit harder each second.

The ball came straight at me. I ran toward it, then stopped. The world started to spin, and I forgot what I was doing.

The ball bounced off the ground, but my thundering heart drowned out its sound.

"Are you all right?" Lori asked me. She was extremely concerned. Mark still hadn't returned to school, and he'd gotten in a lot of trouble with his parents. And I could tell she knew I was stoned.

I couldn't answer. *She knows I'm still doing it.* Those thoughts added to my paranoia. My heart was beating so fast it felt like it was being dribbled by a Harlem Globetrotter. The security lady stared at me suspiciously, causing my anxiety to skyrocket.

As my stress level rose, I spaced out even more until the world seemed completely surreal — like I was a ghost standing among live people.

One by one, the other students noticed something was wrong. I felt their eyes on me from every direction.

"Come on," the security lady said, grabbing my arm. "You need to see the nurse."

She led me out of the gym and down a corridor of wavering fluorescent lights. Everything looked distant somehow. The walls passed by like a pulsating cartoon background. My feet glided over the ground, and I couldn't feel my footsteps.

By the time I reached the principal's office, I was thoroughly freaked out.

"Did you set fire to the bathroom?" the principal demanded.

"No," I answered, but I fought back a panic attack as I realized that I was carrying a lighter on me.

"Search his pockets," he snapped.

That was the last thing in the world I wanted to hear. If they found the lighter, I'd be dead meat. They already knew I'd been on a hall pass to go to the bathroom when the fire was started. They would certainly pin an arson charge on me.

"Stand up," the vice principal commanded.

I was so nervous that I sprang to my feet. But my blood pressure was so high that I became dizzy. The world spun, and I swooned to the side. I barely managed to keep from collapsing.

"Call an ambulance!" yelled the nurse.

Someone guided me back into the chair. "Stay relaxed, Ryan."

The lunch bell rang, dismissing the students into the hallway. There was no way to hide what was going on. No doubt, the news of my overdose had already made it out of gym class and was spreading through the rest of the school.

The world spun, and I collapsed, unable to talk. Paramedics rushed into the office and strapped me onto a gurney. They rolled me past more than 100 students, teachers and faculty as they took me to the ambulance.

At the hospital, they pumped charcoal dust and water into my stomach in order to soak up some of the unabsorbed drugs. They pumped my stomach and monitored my heart rate.

With a clipboard in his hands, the doctor asked me a long list of questions. Then he discharged me.

I was suspended from school until I completed a drug counseling program and a psychological evaluation, neither of which I ever intended to do. I convinced my parents I didn't need either.

So I hung around the house pretending that I needed "recovery time" until I got a phone call several days later. It was from Mark.

"This is totally the bomb! You know DXM, the active ingredient in Coricidin? It's in Robitussin Cough Gels! And Robitussin doesn't have any blood pressure ingredients! Which means —"

"— no seizures or heart attacks!" I finished. A wave of excitement spread through my entire body. *I could get high again without the risks!*

"Dude, we need to get down to Safeway and get some of that!"

Less than 10 minutes later, Lori swung by my house, and we were streaking down the road, tires screeching.

"Where's Mark?"

"He's under a parental version of house arrest. Seriously, they'll kill him if he goes anywhere. So we'll have to bring it to him."

We stole enough for the three of us and several others. By the time we got to Mark's house, I was already stoned.

I started with 10 gel caps, but it wasn't long before my tolerance rose and I needed 20. And then 30. And 40. And as I used more pills, my stealing habits increased in brashness and frequency. I headed to just about every store that stocked Robitussin, taking as much as I could get away with.

***

For the rest of my 10th grade year, I continued to live with my parents, convincing them that my drug use was just a short phase. Nothing but an ignorant teen experiment. I'd learned my lesson. I was now completely and forever clean.

They actually believed me.

Their trust gave me something to manipulate. Instead of giving up drugs, my usage only increased. I'd go on walks during the day, always with the same purpose — to get drugs. I was always stoned by the time I got back. And this became my new routine. Get stoned, study, go steal drugs, come home, get more stoned, go steal drugs, get more stoned, come home, lie to my parents that I was sober, get stoned, go to bed — wash, rinse, repeat.

But my parents weren't fooled as easily as I thought.

One evening, when I was on my way back home from Fred Meyer, a chain store that stocked Robitussin, I saw an odd car parked in our driveway. I knew something was amiss, but I tried to walk in the front door as if I wasn't high.

"Where were you?" my mother asked. She was sitting in the living room with my father and two people I barely knew: Joseph and Julie, a Christian couple who attended my parents' church.

"I was just out walking."

"Were you stealing drugs?"

That question slammed me in the gut, but I answered like a pro. "No."

"Don't lie."

"I'm not."

My mother sighed. "The Lord told me you were at Fred Meyer stealing drugs, so I went down there and checked their cameras. I saw you, Ryan." My mother started to cry. "Oh, Ryan. I don't know what to do with you."

My father interjected. "We've done everything we could. So we called Joseph and Julie. They're going to tell you what you need to do. And you better do what they say."

"There's somewhere you need to go, Ryan," said Joseph. "It's for your own good. To help you get those demons off your back."

His wife continued. "It'll help you get control of your drug use. You want that, don't you? To have your family respect you again?"

The place they brought me to was a lockdown rehab clinic. I kept thinking to myself, *I only started with pills several months ago. How did I end up someplace like this so fast?* Everyone being admitted was thoroughly searched to make sure he didn't sneak in any drugs.

And despite my pleas, my parents were adamant that I'd make it through the detox program with no prescriptions of any kind. But one week after I arrived, the hospital admitted another patient, as well. Roy.

"Check it out, man," he said. He pulled a bottle from inside his shirt and showed it to me. It was a prescription bottle. "Oxycodone," he bragged. "I got them past everyone. There are 20 of 'em."

The pill bottle drew me like a moth to flame. "Come on. Give me 10."

"No way. These are all I've got."

"If you give me half, I won't tell anybody you have them."

"I didn't have to tell you."

"But you did. Come on, fork up." I pretended to call for the nurse.

He grimaced. "Quiet! Okay, okay. Jerk." He reluctantly complied. As soon as he left, I swallowed three.

I'd never taken an opiate before and as such, had no idea that it was dangerous to take them on an empty stomach. My stomach acid started to bubble like a mini volcano, so when lunchtime came, I ate as much as I could to try and settle my stomach. Eating turned out to be a big mistake. The food had the opposite effect I'd intended. It only added pressure to my stomach and helped activate more of the opiate-acid interaction.

I doubled over in sheer agony. The nurses quickly escorted me to their emergency room where a doctor strode in. His face was stern and bore a dour expression.

"Why are you sick? Did you eat something?"

My stomach twisted, and I felt so sick I thought I was going to die. "I took these pills," I gasped. I pulled out the remaining seven tablets and handed them to the doctor.

"Where did you get these?" he demanded, grabbing my collar and shaking me.

I was in so much agony that I couldn't endure the interrogation. "Roy," I answered.

I didn't realize it at the time, but the hospital could've been in a lot of trouble for allowing me access to drugs. They hadn't checked Roy as thoroughly as they should have, and if my parents decided to sue, the hospital might have been liable for a huge amount of money.

That was why they were so harsh with me. But at the time, all I could think of was what death would be like — how merciful it would feel if my gut didn't feel like a live volcano.

They locked me in a confinement ward where I couldn't interact with anybody but doctors and nurses. Then, a bit shy of two weeks later, a different doctor walked into the room. "Your insurance has expired. Pack your things."

I expected to return home, but my parents had another idea. They utilized some contacts in our church and arranged a meeting with the Northwest Mission Bible Training Course. It was an outreach program that helped drug addicts recover and get their lives right with Jesus. They only enrolled people who were 18 or older, but after hearing my story, they decided to allow me an admissions interview. I became the youngest person ever admitted into the program.

It started with a two-month blackout period in which I wasn't allowed to talk to anybody outside of the center. All I was supposed to do was learn about Jesus, gain discipline and stay clean.

I did all three for a while, but after the first two weeks, once I wasn't supervised so closely, I snuck out of the center, headed to the nearest convenience store, stole a few packs of Robitussin and proceeded to get completely stoned.

I continued with the program, making progress for a few days, then failing again as I snuck out and got high. The program wasn't working, so I decided to quit the following morning.

The night before I quit, one of the senior students visited me.

"God just spoke to me," he said somberly. "He wants me to tell you that if you quit this program, you're going to keep ending up in programs exactly like this until you finally complete one."

I listened to his words, and chills raced through my body. But I'd already made up my mind. The following day, I went home.

My mother was so disappointed in me that she cried like I'd never seen before. I couldn't bear it, so I wrote a note to ease her grief:

If I screw up even once, I'll go back to the Northwest Mission Bible Training Course. Ryan Smith

She so desperately wanted to hold onto any thread of hope that she decided to believe the letter.

***

I stayed clean for a month, after which my parents sat me down and told me I had to go back to school. My mother had started working and had neither the time nor the energy to home school me. And they couldn't watch my behavior while they were both at work.

I begged them to let me stay home and study for my GED. Once again, I fooled them by doing the minimum. And I took more and more drugs.

As soon as I turned 16, I took the examination and was awarded my GED.

Now, I didn't have to worry about going back to school. My life was fully my own. I was finally free.

COMING HOME

But my brother didn't see it that way. "What are you doing with your life?" he asked. I was in the kitchen, eating an over-stacked ham sandwich, stoned out of my mind when my brother stormed in and started to vent. "Do you think you're being cool or something? What is your *problem*? Can't you see how messed up you are?"

I wasn't used to my brother confronting me like this, and the rage came through me faster than I expected. I stood up and grabbed a knife from the drawer. A moment later, we were tussling. He tripped backward, and I sprang on top of him and brought the knife down —

It *thunked* into the floor next to his ear.

"Don't you ever yell at me!" I said. "I'll kill you!"

My mother ran into the kitchen and screamed. A moment later, she picked up the phone and three minutes later, a police car pulled up, lights blazing.

They charged me with reckless endangerment.

I didn't care.

My next three years consisted of a worsening cycle of jail, overdoses, rehab clinics, counseling, psyche wards, back to jail, more overdoses and more rehab — the pattern seemed unbreakable. I didn't really want it to change, either. I ended up in the hospital virtually every week and became so well acquainted with the charcoal stomach pump that I tasted it in my sleep. I was a text-book hard case junkie.

Somewhere in that dirty cycle, I was exposed to tuberculosis, and although I didn't contract it, I was given a one-year supply of Isoniazid in order to prevent the illness from manifesting. I had to get regular toxicity checks to make sure my organs weren't being overtaxed as Isoniazid was highly damaging to the liver. The doctor who prescribed it went to great lengths to warn me not to take more than the prescribed dose and never to take it with alcohol. This drug had no "junky-favored" side effects, only the certainty of causing liver damage.

Finally, I turned 18, and I had nowhere to go. I was legally a man, so I couldn't go back to juvie. My parents wouldn't let me come home (I didn't blame them), but they did find a Christian gentleman who'd let me stay with him — provided I stayed clean and worked to earn my keep.

JOURNEY TOWARD FREEDOM

His name was Ray Farmer, and he was such a stabilizing influence that I managed to stay clean when I was working with him and living at his house. He talked to me every day about Jesus, character and being a good Christian. And he lived by every word he spoke. I didn't deserve all of his kindness, but that didn't stop me from disappointing him. Little by little, I started doing drugs again. At first, I was able to hide it from him, but he caught wind of it. He prayed with me every day, putting all his heart and soul into petitioning God on my behalf. And most importantly, he convinced me to rededicate my life to Christ.

Christmas approached, and I asked my parents if I could stay with them once again.

"Ryan," my mother said, "you're not allowed here anymore, and you know it."

It hurt not being allowed to see my family, even during the holiday. "Please," I begged. "I really want to change. I promise."

She reluctantly gave in.

But on Christmas Day, I stole a bottle of vodka, drank it and passed out on the couch. That was the last straw — my mother told me to leave.

Ray Farmer picked me up and took me to breakfast. Rain beat on the large restaurant windows, reminding me of how fast my heart had beaten so many times. Over plates of eggs and pancakes, Ray admonished me. "You're ruining peoples' lives besides your own," he said harshly. The change in his demeanor caught me off guard. I didn't know how to handle it. He'd always been so kind to me that this switch was more than I could take.

"You need to get right with the Lord. You're wasting every bit of grace you've been given, and it's closing in on the time that you won't be given any more chances. Once everybody gives up on you, it's over. So many people have bent over backward to help you, and you've slapped them all in the face. And you don't even want to admit that anything is wrong. Honestly, you need to be ashamed of your behavior."

He leaned over the table and looked me straight in the eye. "Ryan, you need to change or you'll end up dead."

I started shaking so badly, I couldn't even hold my silverware. My anger welled up until I couldn't bear to look at Ray.

"I don't need you!" I yelled. "I never asked for this!" I stood up and stormed out of the restaurant. Two minutes later, I'd already stolen a bottle of wine from a convenience store and went to work taking the rest of my Isoniazid. All 100 pills.

Rain cascaded from the dreary sky, and blackness closed in on my soul. I staggered to a tree and lay down in the mud at its base. My vision blurred, my heart rate slowed. I felt death come and welcomed it with open arms.

***

But as everything faded, light rushed into me. I was overcome with a desire to live.

The light guided my vision to a church at the top of a hill. I could barely make it out through the trees, but it literally glowed, beckoning me like a lighthouse in the darkness. I knew I needed to get there or I'd certainly die.

One hand forward, one knee ahead — I crawled up the wet, muddy hill doing everything I could to keep the church in my sight. My eyelids weighed a thousand pounds each, and my heart felt like it had turned into grime. I couldn't throw up even though my stomach twisted, causing me to dry heave hundreds of times in succession.

My left hand clawed the earth. Then my right. The rain pounded on my back, filling me with numbness and chills. Everything grew dim. My eyesight faded. But still, my fingers dug ahead as if on their own accord.

I headed toward the light.

By the time I reached the church steps, something seemed to lift me. I was able to climb to my feet and pull myself through the door.

Someone inside said, "Oh, my Lord," but I couldn't make her features out.

"Call 911." They were the only words I could muster before I collapsed to the ground.

The police showed up right behind me. Ray Farmer had been concerned that I might kill myself, and he'd called them. Like always, Ray proved to be right. And I'd let him down again. I'd let my family down. I'd let everybody down.

I fell into a seizure.

Hectic yells. Quick orders. An ambulance. Straps. Rising. Flashing lights. A siren.

JOURNEY TOWARD FREEDOM

All the while, I'd turned into an earthquake — my spiritual fault lines had broken, and my body was caught in uncontrollable tremors.

"He's not going to make it."

My heart exploded.

Pain. Spinning. Blackness.

***

I woke up in Oregon Health & Science University Hospital, the premier hospital in the region for intensive care and specialist treatments. Against all odds, I was alive. But only by a thread.

After at least a dozen tests, the specialists concluded that the damage to my liver was so severe that it probably wouldn't recover. They started looking for possible donors. But each day, my readings improved as my liver miraculously began to heal. And a quiet voice kept speaking to me, telling me what I needed to do in order to live.

"I need help," I told the doctor. "I need to go to Freedom House."

Strangely enough, speaking those words felt real to me. As a consummate liar, it had become hard for me to discern when I was telling the truth or not. But I actually believed I needed to change — I was actually scared. My defiant spirit was breaking.

"You shouldn't be alive," a doctor told me. "You must have someone watching over you because you did so much damage to yourself that your organs should have simply shut down. You had a massive heart attack. It was drug induced, so at least you don't have any tissue damage. But unless you stay clean, you're likely to have more. You're out of control, Ryan. Do yourself a favor. Get some serious help, or you'll end up dead in a gutter someplace."

After they discharged me, I decided to truly get help. There was no way I could recover on my own. The demons of addiction were too strong for me, so I sold my Xbox 360 to pay the admission to Freedom House.

Jim, one of the leaders, interviewed me on a Friday afternoon and, after a grueling question and answer session, reluctantly agreed to take me in. He'd heard about my history but was still willing to give me a final chance.

Once more, my life hung by a thread.

"If you're serious, you should start right now," Jim explained. "I'll make room for you."

"Please, just let me come in on Monday. I need to see my family this one last time before doing this."

"Procrastination isn't change, Ryan. If you truly want it, you'll start right away."

"I just — I really need to see my family. I'll stay clean. I mean it. I can't do this without saying goodbye to my family."

He stared at me for a long time before speaking. "This is against my better judgment, but we can't make you do anything you don't want to. Stay clean through Monday."

"I will," I promised. And I actually believed myself.

***

At home, I stayed clean for the first day, but the second day, I succumbed to temptation and decided to get high *just one last time*. I took 80 pills before heading back to my parents' house. When I walked in the door, everything was quiet. Nobody was there except me. I was relieved for a second, but a huge, dark presence engulfed me.

It was as if God lifted his protection from me. A malignant darkness came into the house, and I was overcome with rage. I kicked the door open and stormed into the garage. My whole world seemed like it had gone up in flames. I thought of the very first thing I'd stolen — the lighter. And it became perfectly clear. When I'd first looked into the flames of that lighter, I'd had a flash of insight.

But now, as hopeless thoughts assailed me from every recess of my brain, I realized how wrong my insight had been. I *couldn't* have anything I wanted simply by taking it. Each time I stole something, a part of me was stolen in return, until I was left so empty inside that I had nothing left. There was only one thing I could think of to do.

Purify with fire!

Burn everything!

I ran to the garage and grabbed a can of gasoline. I doused the outside of the house, then carried the can inside and splattered gas through the hallway, up the stairs and finally into my parents' room. Gas fumes filled the air as I kicked open the closet that housed my father's guns. I picked up a .380 semiautomatic pistol, loaded it and started shooting into the gas spills.

The bullets should have been hot enough to ignite the gasoline, but they didn't. Something screamed inside me — *Stop this! This isn't what you should be doing! You need to get help!*

It felt like I was watching someone else's movie unfold. I was the cameraman filming the drama. I put the gun to my own head and started to squeeze the trigger.

A voice spoke to me. It was the senior student from Northwest Mission Bible Training Course — the one who visited me the night before I quit.

"*God just spoke to me,*" he said somberly. "*He wants me to tell you that if you quit this program, you're going to keep ending up in programs exactly like this until you finally complete one.*"

But before I could think, another voice cut into my head. *Burn everything! Kill yourself!*

A kinder voice said, *Ryan, this isn't the end. I'm here. I'll always be here for you.*

Trembling, I lowered the gun. Almost on its own accord, my hand picked up the phone and dialed 911.

"I've just soaked my house with gasoline ... and I have a loaded gun. I've been shooting things ... *I need help.*"

Every available police car in town showed up, lights blazing. The police swarmed in like a swat team. I stood there, pointing the pistol at the floor as they tazed me to the ground.

First a hospital, then a high-security psyche ward. The whole time I kept asking to go to Freedom House, but my requests fell on deaf ears.

It took my probation officer, my family, their friends and church members and many desperate phone calls for Freedom House to agree to give me one final chance.

This was it. My last chance for life.

The psyche ward was only too happy to get rid of me. I lied to everyone and managed to break out several times, get stoned and even bring drugs back in. But each time I broke out, it hurt inside, and I knew I shouldn't be doing it. I knew I was sinking lower each time.

They wanted to get rid of me so badly they even provided a van to transport me away — to help me become someone else's headache. The van's driver had no idea what kind of manipulative junky I was. So, as we drove past a Safeway, I decided to get high *just one last time.*

"Just stop here for a second. I need to pick something up."

The driver pulled into the parking lot. I walked inside as if I had no intention of doing anything wrong. But old habits die hard, and I took 60 Robitussin tablets in the bathroom, then stole a bottle of Pepsi to make the driver think that was what I'd stopped for.

By the time we reached Freedom House, I was spinning out of my mind.

I strode in, trying to hide the fact that I was stoned. But Jim's eyes cut past my façade like a hot knife through butter. He sat me down in his office and leaned forward on his desk.

"Freedom House is no longer an option for you," he stated. His words sounded like a judge giving a verdict. "You've done a great job fooling everybody, and I think you're trying to fool us again. You've blown every chance everyone has ever given you, and there's nothing more we can do for you. You'll have to look elsewhere. I mean, look at you — you're even stoned right now!"

"Please!" My heart felt like a broken drum. "There is nowhere else. I promise you I really want to change this time. I mean it! Freedom House is my only hope."

Jim stared at me for a long time. His eyes seemed to bore into my soul, searching for any sign of falsehood. I stared at him with desperation, hoping he could sense my intense desire to make it work. Deep down, I knew that the chance someone would believe in me was almost nonexistent. I'd burned every single bridge I had, betraying and lying to every person in my life.

I couldn't meet his eyes. As he stared, my life flashed back to me. Every wrong thing I'd done fell onto my soul like a thousand tons of nails. I was cut, battered, broken. And I needed help.

God, I prayed silently, *I need you in this moment. You said you'll always be here for me. Please. You're all I've got left. God, I need you in this moment.*

I must have prayed the same thing more than 20 times. I had to make absolutely certain that God heard me. I felt like I was 7 years old again, asking Jesus to come into my life. But back then, I didn't truly know how much I needed him. Now, I needed Jesus more than I needed air.

Finally, Jim's posture softened and he spoke. "You'll have an accountability partner — which means 24-hour monitoring — for your first two weeks. Honestly, Ryan, I don't expect you'll make it."

I was so relieved, I started to cry.

"And, Ryan," Jim continued, "this will truly be your last chance. I mean it. If it turns out you're fooling me, you're on your own."

***

The first two weeks were hard, but I knew I was where I was supposed to be. Something inside me had broken, and I was finally ready to change. The schedule was strict and like Jim promised, there was always someone watching me.

Every day, we prayed, did devotions and studied the principles of God, Jesus and the Holy Spirit. We worked three hours every day, Monday through Saturday, and spent most of Sunday praying, attending service and taking time to meditate upon God. And there was always an assignment looming over us.

The most difficult assignment was to write a letter to my family. Writing the letter wasn't like anything I'd ever done before. No matter how desperately I wanted to tell them that everything would be okay, I didn't. I knew my words were thin, and I needed to write things they'd believe. So I wrote a long apology for all the things I'd done and the ways I'd hurt my family so many times.

I was surprised to tears when I received a letter from my family. It was short, and I could tell by the handwriting that it was written with a shaking hand, but their closing words showed me how much they loved me, despite all the hurt I'd put them through.

Ryan, we're behind you 100 percent.

I cried until I was completely exhausted. My family's love convicted me of so many things I'd done. I couldn't believe how they could still want me to do well — I'd hurt them so much year after year. I'd never done anything to earn that kind of love. And I knew that I couldn't disappoint them again. Something inside me had finally changed.

After two months in Freedom House, I was still clean.

My parents came to my Level 1 graduation. I saw hope and trust return to their eyes, and for the first time in my life, I felt like I'd truly earned something. I hadn't tricked anyone. I'd fought hard and stayed clean. I'd done everything I was supposed to. And I was more proud of becoming a Level 2 than I was of anything else I'd ever done.

Little by little, I learned to accept correction and see the staff differently. God revealed that they were there to help me, and their criticism was for my own good. It was hard to stomach at first, but after several months, I lost my resentment and started to appreciate the help.

I graduated from Level 2 and became a Level 3.

I was growing stronger every day, strengthened by the godly men who sacrificed so much of themselves to minister to me. I'd never stuck to anything this long in my life, and there was nothing that was going to make me quit. Not when I was so close to true freedom — the kind that comes from love, discipline and submission to God's will.

Shortly after, my parents lifted the restraining order against me. And even though I could go home, I had no desire to quit the program. I knew I was right where I was supposed to be, and nothing in the world was going to take me from the place God had made for me.

And I know the next time I step through the door to my house, I'll have tears in my eyes. Because this time, I'll finally be the person I'm meant to be — the kind of son my parents can be proud of. I'll finally be walking step by step with Jesus.

I'll finally be home.

FREEDOM ROAD
The Story of Phillip Koglin
Written by Karen Koczwara

"Oh, s***. This is bad." The chilly winter air whipped at my shoulders as I hunkered down behind the rusted garbage can. In the dim streetlight, I caught sight of the ugly abscess on my upper leg. It wasn't the first time I'd seen it, but it had grown significantly in the past few days. Shuddering, I yanked up my tattered pants to take a better look. "This is bad, really bad." Gingerly, I touched it as though it were a dead, rotting animal.

How did I get here? Again? I leaned back against the cold metal garbage can and peeled a half-brown banana I'd found inside. The mushy flesh of the fruit did little to fill my stomach, but I reasoned it was safer than the half-eaten hamburger I'd eaten last night. What sort of life was this, anyway? Hiding behind garbage cans, digging through trash bags, always running?

My thin flannel shirt, the only shirt I owned, clung to my back, stale with perspiration and dirt. I hadn't showered in weeks but didn't care. Life on the streets didn't require polished shoes, a pressed suit or gourmet dinners. I tossed the banana peel back in the garbage and peered up at the dark sky above. Thick black clouds now hung perilously over me, announcing a heavy storm just minutes from now. I was all too familiar with the rainy Portland nights. If I were lucky, I would find shelter tonight at the local shooting gallery.

The abscess rubbed against my pants, a nasty reminder that I desperately needed medical help. I closed my eyes and took a deep breath. A second gale of wind stung my cheeks, and a wave of nausea washed over me. The ache in the pit of my stomach was a mixture of physical and emotional pain. Was it worth the trip across town in this nasty weather to find help? Or was I better off lying here behind the garbage can where death could find me a bit more easily?

Death. Maybe I *was* better off dead. At least there would be no more running. Death was a fresh start, an almost welcome option for a very desperate man at the end of his rope ...

JOURNEY TOWARD FREEDOM

***

"Phillip, I'm off to work. You know the drill." My mother popped her head into my bedroom, car keys jangling in her hand. "Behave, all right?"

"Yeah." I yanked the covers over my head to keep out the bright sunlight that streamed through my window. I didn't care to get up this morning. Everything would be the same today. I'd go to school, come home to an empty house, rummage around for something to eat and wait for Mom and Curtis to return from work. Curtis started work as a painter every morning at 4 a.m. with a drink to get him going. He drank throughout the day and then would begin drinking when he got home. Just like clockwork. Mom would arrive home later and often join him. And she would get very mean as she drank. It was a regular routine.

Yeah, I knew the drill all right, and I wasn't sure it was worth waking up for.

Reluctantly, I pulled myself out of bed and yanked on some clothes. I peered out the window, thankful for the rare sunny Oregon day. Good weather meant I got to kick the ball around on the soccer field after school. Sports kept me busy, kept me from remembering that life at home wasn't so great.

An only child, my parents had divorced when I was just 1 year old. My mother remarried a man named Curtis when I was 3. Curtis, better known as "Crazy Curtis" by his motorcycle buddies, was a raging alcoholic. He lured my mother into his little world in no time.

I saw my biological father every other weekend. He was an alcoholic, as well. Scattered beer cans and empty liquor bottles became household decorations in and around his home. I often felt out of place, a third wheel wherever I went. It seemed the minute the booze came out, I became quickly forgotten, an afterthought in the lives of my less-than-sober parents.

School provided an outlet for me, a place of refuge where I could shine. I got good grades and threw myself into a variety of sports, from soccer to baseball to chess. My athletic build made me a natural. I loved the thrill of making a goal or batting in a run on the ball field. People cheered and clapped, and for a moment, I was the center of the world. But the boy who shone on the field just as quickly disappeared the minute he got home.

FREEDOM ROAD

One afternoon, a boy in my fifth grade class pulled me aside before recess. "I got somethin' to show you. Meet me out on the field," he whispered, patting his pants pocket.

I tried my first cigarette that day behind the bushes on the school field. The smoke burned my lungs a bit, but I felt like a rebel on a mission as we hunkered down taking long drags and exhaling. I had a feeling this wouldn't be my last smoke.

From fifth grade on, I continued to smoke cigarettes. Stealing them from my parents was easier than expected. I figured my mom would never notice the smell, since her own clothes reeked of smoke.

Across town, my grandparents led a starkly different lifestyle than the one I knew at home. Both devout Christians, their lives revolved around going to church and serving the Lord. I often visited their home on the weekends and enjoyed the time I spent there. The peaceful environment was a far cry from the crazy, drunken one I lived in.

My grandpa Jim was a great role model, living life as a godly man, and I especially appreciated the way he did everything he could to be my fishing buddy. My grandmother Bonnie was a wonderful woman who loved God greatly. She practically glowed with happiness. I loved the attention she lavished on me, the way her kind, bubbly voice spilled over as she read to me from her old leather Bible.

"I have a little song I want to sing for you," Grandma told me one night as she tucked me in. "It's called 'The B-I-B-L-E.' Have you ever heard it before?"

I shook my head. "No. Will you sing it for me?"

"The B-I-B-L-E, yes, that's the book for me; I stand alone on the word of God, the B-I-B-L-E." Her voice rang out like an angel's as she sung the snappy tune. "It's a good reminder that we can always count on God's word for our everyday needs. Whatever we need, it's all in this book. Isn't that wonderful?"

I blinked and nodded. "Yeah." I loved the way my grandmother's eyes lit up, the corners creasing just a bit, when she smiled. She was so different from my mother, whose eyes were always sad or angry or just plain distant. I pulled the cool sheets up to my chin and closed my eyes. How I loved my grandmother's house with its cheery décor and tidy little room set up just for me. Here, I was not forgotten. Here, I was safe and loved.

JOURNEY TOWARD FREEDOM

"Would you like to go to Sunday school tomorrow?" she asked, planting a kiss on my cheek.

I nodded. "Yes!" I replied eagerly. I loved going to church. It was a rare, special treat like having ice cream for dinner. The Sunday school teacher talked about the love Jesus had for every girl and boy. I often wondered if she really meant *every* girl and boy. *Even the ones who smoked cigarettes behind the school at recess?*

As I proceeded through middle school, I quickly found that the key to popularity was drinking and smoking. I graduated from cigarettes to marijuana and enjoyed the quick high I got from a joint. I was surprised at how easy it was to obtain the drug and just how many people smoked it. By seventh grade, I had tried nearly every type of hard liquor and was hooked on pot.

I continued to get good grades in school and kept up a good front at home. I probably could have come home with a shaved head and gone unnoticed, as my parents were too busy drinking. Most evenings, Curtis stumbled into the living room after work, ripped off his painter pants and began to unwind in his usual way, which always seemed to include hard liquor. An hour later, he'd pass out in front of the television. On more than one occasion, I threw keg parties when no one else was home. This made me even more popular with my peers. Life was good, or so I thought.

By the eighth grade, my mother divorced Curtis, claiming she could no longer deal with his crazy ways. I wondered if a sense of peace might return to our home, but our lives became even more insane.

"Phillip, we're going to the dog races!" My mother yanked the covers off of me one Saturday morning and threw my winter coat at me.

The dog races, it turned out, were lots of fun. My mother showed me how to read a spreadsheet, and I quickly caught on. Adrenaline pumped through my veins as the dogs lapped around the arena while fans cheered from the stands. When my mother collected a hefty chunk of change at the end of the evening, I was impressed. Maybe this gambling business wasn't so bad after all.

My mother went from gambling at dog races to gambling in Reno and Las Vegas. On the morning of my 12th birthday, I awoke to find that she was gone. A short note on the kitchen table was the only gift I got: *Phillip, went to Vegas. Be back tomorrow morning. Love, Mom.* My mother had missed my birthday because she'd gone off to gamble! On second thought, maybe gambling wasn't a friend after all.

My mother moved us in with my grandparents, claiming it would be a more wholesome environment. I was thrilled with the living situation. I missed Mom a bit when she was gone, but smoking pot and drinking helped ease that loneliness I felt at home.

By the end of eighth grade, I had worked my way up to heavier drugs like cocaine, acid and mushrooms. There wasn't a drug I tried that wasn't my friend. I loved "tripping" and found that the more drugs I did, the more popular I became.

One afternoon, right after I ate some acid, I was called into the school office. "Your great-grandfather is sick," the receptionist explained. "Stay here until a family member can pick you up."

I thought this was a bit odd, but didn't think much of it. My grandpa Jim arrived and said little as we picked up Mom and headed out of town.

As the miles passed, I had a hunch something was suspicious but being loaded on acid, I couldn't be sure.

"Where are we really going?" I asked.

My mother raised her brow. "You're not well, son. You need help."

Help? I was only 14 years old. How did my mother know I needed help? I thought I had hid my habits so well.

"Where are you taking me?" I demanded, raising my voice.

Mom said nothing, and within minutes, we pulled into a drug treatment center. My heart lurched as she opened the car door for me.

"You'll thank me for this later," she muttered.

Reluctantly, I dragged my feet into the center. After checking in, I received a physical. The doctor's words nearly shocked me out of my socks.

"Your kidneys are bleeding," the doctor said somberly.

My kidneys were bleeding?! This was not good news. I knew my drug activity had increased substantially, but I had no idea I had been damaging my body.

I met with a drug counselor the next morning. He took a long swig of his coffee as he spoke to me. "Phillip, let me tell you something. I'm addicted to coffee. I can't stop drinking it. I need my fix every morning or I get pretty cranky. I suppose you feel this way about drugs. Am I right?"

I shrugged. How could he compare a stupid cup of coffee with drugs?

Unfortunately, the treatment center made little impact on me. I became an expert ping-pong player but got little else out of it. After leaving the center, I went back to live with my mother, who had moved in with her new boyfriend a few miles out of town. I continued drinking and smoking pot on a regular basis.

By the time I reached my junior year in high school, I decided school was not worth attending. My studies got in the way of my drinking time, and I didn't like this. The school and I both seemed to agree that it would be best if I did not return.

When I was 17 years old, I moved in with my biological father, whom I'd seen little of during my childhood years. I obtained my driver's license and got a job at the Oregon Catholic Press. Having my first real job with the printers' union was exciting. Who needed school when there was good money to be made in the real world?

The living situation with my father was less than ideal, however. He had remarried and had three boys with his new wife. Having been an only child my whole life, the idea of siblings didn't excite me. I spent most days working and hanging out with my new girlfriend, which helped take my mind off things at home.

One day, my girlfriend came to me in tears. She was shaking so badly she could hardly speak. "I'm pregnant, Phillip," she whispered. "I don't know what to do."

My girlfriend already had a child from a previous relationship. Neither of us was ready to be parents to a new baby. My heart sank as I fumbled for words. "I'll help you, um, take care of it if you want to."

She nodded and stared at the ground. "Thanks," she muttered through her tears. "That would be nice."

And so my very first paycheck went to pay for an abortion. I felt terrible about the situation but didn't know what else to do. That decision still haunts me to this day.

One summer day, I came home to find two large garbage bags on the front porch. I was appalled to see all of my belongings inside. Everything from my clothes to my drug paraphernalia had been thrown into them — my entire life reduced to two garbage bags.

Furious, I reached inside and pulled out one of my only nice shirts. It was stained with tobacco juice, which had spilled out of one of my pipes. Tears burning my eyes, I cursed under my breath. How could my family do this to me?

I went to live with my uncle Eddie, who also worked at the Catholic Press. He was a recovering alcoholic and was sympathetic to my situation. "Just don't make no trouble around here, and everything will be cool, all right?" he told me.

I nodded gratefully. "Yes, sir," I replied.

It didn't take long for me to disappoint him. One weekend when my uncle was out of town, I called everyone I knew and invited them over for a party. A few hours later, my uncle's large house was filled with dozens of people ready to have a good time. The booze and the drugs appeared, and the hoopla commenced. I drank myself right into a blackout.

The next thing I remembered was waking up on my girlfriend's couch. My grandma was there and visibly upset. She was asking me all about how I could have trashed and flooded my uncle's house. With my mind clouded, I couldn't even begin to know what she was talking about. I ended up going over to my uncle's when he was gone and cleaning up one of the biggest disasters I helped create but knew absolutely nothing about. And as for my friends, no one came by to help.

Obviously, I was no longer welcome there, and I suspected that treatment appeared to be just ahead.

I was terribly upset, not because my friends had trashed his house, but because I had been caught and kicked out. With that bridge burned, I wondered where I would go next. Thankfully, my grandparents took me back in under the condition that I enter a treatment program. I went reluctantly because I did not want to be on the streets.

One afternoon, on my way to a basketball game at New Hope Community Church, I passed a flattened Bronco truck. I shuddered as I glanced over at the shattered windows and crumpled frame. It looked like my friend Kelly's truck. Surely, it couldn't be!

Later that afternoon, I returned home and found my family seated quietly in the living room. My mother looked up at me with somber eyes. "Your friends were in a terrible car accident today, Phillip. Derrik is dead, and Kelly is in critical condition."

I stared at my mother, watching her mouth move but not believing the words coming out. Dead? My childhood friend was dead?

JOURNEY TOWARD FREEDOM

"You're kidding, right?" I asked, sinking to the floor.

My mother shook her head. "I wish I were."

I should have been in that car, I thought, a wave of nausea washing over me. Had it been any other day, I would have been in that car with my buddies. To think my friend was dead, and it could have been me. I shuddered, too horrified to speak.

The news shook me up terribly, but it didn't stop me from drinking and doing drugs. I did discover a new best friend: Vicodin. It was easy to get my hands on and felt great mixed with a few beers.

I soon began dating a girl I'd known from middle school, Misty. We shared the same birthday and soon found out we had many other things in common. I fell in love, or what I thought was love. We moved in together, and the partying continued.

Though I managed to keep up my job at the printing press, the rest of my life began crumbling. I was miserable, trying to fill my emptiness with drugs and booze. On the outside, I looked like I had my act together. I kept up with sports, made decent money and had a pretty girl on my arm. But inside, I was hopelessly adrift and miserable.

When I turned 21, I went to Las Vegas for the first time. Instantly, I fell in love with the bright lights, poker tables and slot machines. It didn't take me long to figure out why they called it Sin City. The days of gambling at the dog races with my mother came back as I hovered around the tables, trying to make a quick buck. I had found another love to compete with my drugs and drinking: gambling. But this new love couldn't comfort me with what was about to happen.

One afternoon, I got horrible news. My precious grandmother was diagnosed with Lou Gehrig's disease. Over the next couple of years, I watched her waste away. Though she was once an active member of her church and the community, now my grandmother couldn't even lift a spoon to her mouth. It broke my heart to watch my grandfather feed her and bathe her as though she were a child. Her tiny frame grew to an emaciated state, and eventually she passed away.

I sobbed for weeks following my grandmother's death.

"How could you let her die, God?" I cried out angrily. "She was a good woman! She didn't deserve this!" I didn't talk to God often, but I still believed he existed, and I wondered how he could have allowed such tragedy. My grandmother was one of the only good things in my life, and now she was gone.

This only made me more bitter and gave me a new excuse to continue drinking and using drugs.

***

Misty and I bought a house and married, but our relationship quickly took a turn for the worse. I got into crystal meth and spent more and more time away from home. My usual 5'10", 200-pound frame whittled down to an emaciated 150 pounds. Misty and I often fought about money, which seemed to be tighter than ever these days. I tried my best to keep my drug addiction from her, but she caught on and confronted me about it several times.

"I know I ain't perfect, but this has got to stop, Phillip!" Misty shouted at me one night after I stumbled home late after work. "We never have any money, and I can't stand living like this. You better get your act together before the baby comes along."

"Baby?" I croaked, sinking onto the couch. "You're pregnant?"

Misty nodded, tears filling her eyes. "Yeah."

"Wow. Oh, man." I wasn't ready to be a father. How could a guy who could hardly stay sober for more than an hour raise a child of his own?

Meanwhile, my mother remarried and was diagnosed with bipolar disorder. She turned "crazy" and often came to our house in the middle of the night, screaming and banging down the door. Now heavily into meth, I often stayed up for days on end and battled with my own crazy behavior. My mother introduced me to a guy who knew how to make meth, and I snuck out late at night to work in his lab. I was fascinated by how he mixed the substances and quickly caught on. *Perhaps I could quit my day job and do this full-time, if the money was good.*

My son, Tyler, was born a few months later. I made it to his birth but missed most of the entire pregnancy because I was out getting high. My relationship with Misty grew more strained. I retreated to the bars after work instead of coming home and was unfaithful to her. On the eve of my son's first birthday, when I should have been cutting cake with him, I was passed out on the bed of another woman. It would come to be one of my biggest regrets in life.

JOURNEY TOWARD FREEDOM

It wasn't long after this that I was introduced to the new love of my life: heroin. Though I had sworn I would never inject myself with drugs, I quickly fell in love with the high it brought me. It was unlike any drug I'd ever tried before. There was no going back now. The needle called to me day and night.

I hit a new low, however, and ended up in a place called Hooper Detox. My body was soused with drugs, and being at Hooper gave me a chance to clean it out. From there, I became involved in a mentor program located downtown in a seedy motel. The environment was crazier than any party I'd ever thrown. A co-ed facility, it revolved around doing more drugs and trying to hook up with the opposite sex.

One night, as I slipped into bed, a parade of cockroaches skittered across the room and under my bed. I felt sick but reasoned I had nowhere else to sleep other than the streets. I graduated from the program and moved on, but it wasn't long before I returned to my old ways.

One afternoon, my grandfather called with more devastating news. "I'm afraid your mother has terminal cancer," he said softly.

"Cancer?" I croaked. My mother had lived a hard life of meth, booze, smoking and mental illness, but cancer seemed unfathomable. I sank to my knees and cried as the words sunk in. My mother passed away about a week before Christmas. Here I was a young man in body but worn out emotionally. I had lost my best friends, my beloved grandma and now my mom.

"God," I cried out, "this stinks, this is so unfair! Where are you and the love I've heard of?" These angry emotions would surface again very soon.

***

"Give me a second chance," I begged Misty one night after leaving the program. "I'm going to get my act together, I promise." I loved Misty, despite what we had both been through. We had a child together, and our relationship deserved another try.

"I dunno, Phillip. You've screwed up real bad," Misty mumbled, frowning.

"This time will be different," I promised. Even as I said the words, I knew I wasn't ready to give up the "other woman" … my drugs. We moved to Vancouver, Washington, and attempted to patch things up. I figured I had nothing to lose by returning to church. Misty and I both decided to go, and so I put in an hour a week at Crossroads Church, where I mumbled a few hymns under my breath and listened to the sermon.

I still wasn't happy with God for taking my grandmother. Deep down, I knew there was a void to be filled in my life, but I wasn't ready to give my life to God.

I found work as a sales representative for a window company. My job entailed going door-to-door, convincing people to give me a few hours of their time so I could show them our fabulous windows. I quickly got promoted to manager in the company. My new job entailed driving my employees around in a van from neighborhood to neighborhood. The business was less than honest, to say the least, but the money was fabulous. The job had another perk, too: I had plenty of time to get my employees high inside the van. This made me even more popular with them. I was living the life. I got paid great money to get high with my buddies.

One morning, my boss came to me with a look on his face that said it all. "I know what you've been up to, Phillip," he said quietly. "Turn in your uniform today. I won't have you doing drugs on the clock." I was devastated; things had been going so smoothly. Now at a new rock bottom, my relationship with Misty continued to go downhill.

After the loss of my job, she came to me in tears. "I can't do this anymore, Phillip. I'm done. For good." The hollow sadness in her eyes said it all. There were no more second chances.

I was still reeling from the loss of my friends, my grandmother, my mom and now I was going to lose my wife and son. Everyone important was being ripped from my life.

Why, God? Why?

I moved in with another heroin addict, and life got even worse. I called my grandfather one afternoon desperate for help. He offered me enough money to get well and, hopefully, enter detox. He begged me to get well. "I've been in your shoes as an alcoholic," he told me sympathetically. "You need help. Don't let this ruin you. You'll lose everything."

In my way of looking at life, I had already lost everything important to me. With my son and wife gone and out of the picture, I had little to live for. I found a new girlfriend who did drugs, and we spent our nights driving around making drug deals.

JOURNEY TOWARD FREEDOM

One morning at nearly 2 a.m., I heard sirens wailing as we pulled out of an apartment complex where we'd delivered meth. My heart caught in my throat. I hated cops. They always meant trouble. I remained calm and pulled over to the side of the road.

"License and registration?" the cop asked, peering into my window.

I fumbled for my registration, which was nowhere to be found. "I, uh, just a minute ..." I mumbled.

"Step out of the car," the cop commanded, his smile disappearing.

I complied, and he quickly found my drug stash in the backseat. He walked back around the car to face me. "Listen here. You tell me the truth about these drugs, and I don't take you to jail tonight, understand? Are they yours?"

I gulped and nodded. "Yeah." What did I have to lose by being honest?

"All right. That's all I needed to know."

I breathed a sigh of relief. I had gotten off this time, but what about the next? Would I be so lucky if I had another run-in with the law? It was an unbelievable break. But I knew I needed help.

I went back to Hooper Detox and then from there to a Salvation Army recovery program my grandfather recommended. A six-month program, it was set up like a work camp for 75 men. I worked my way up to a desk job there and began attending church twice a week as a requirement of the program. It made little impact on me. Heroin, speed and meth were only a phone call away anytime I wanted them.

Once out of the program, I continued doing drugs. I spent the next few months in and out of detox, which never did seem to do any good. The only thing I learned inside these places was how to sharpen my game. Not wanting to end up on the streets, I played along with the games of deception for as long as I could.

One afternoon, I locked myself in the bathroom at the Salvation Army center where I managed to keep my job as a thrift store clerk. I shot some heroin and waited for it to kick in. I was now used to shooting dope wherever I went and had learned to mask my habit quite well at work.

When I opened the door, a marshal stood before me, badge in hand. "We have a warrant for your arrest," he said bluntly, looking me up and down. "You been doing drugs in here, son?"

I nodded. There was no use denying it. I'd been caught. "Yes, sir."

The marshal patted me down, found my stash and promptly flushed it. "You're looking at a felony with jail time. Now come with me," he said roughly, jerking my arm.

I spent a few days in the county jail, which made the seedy hotels I'd stayed in look like Buckingham Palace. Hard, cold floors served as my bed, and small, bland meals were my sustenance. I lay there, alone, afraid, with only one thought on my mind: How could I get my next fix? It was a new low for me, but times were only about to get tougher.

After I got out of jail, I lost my job at the Salvation Army and ended up on the streets. I had never thought things would come to this: wandering around downtown Portland in the middle of the night with only the clothes on my back. I prayed each night the rain would stay at bay and rummaged through garbage cans in search of something to eat.

I found work at a mattress shop and earned an easy $80 a day delivering mattresses. The cash, of course, went straight to my dope habit. Meanwhile, my new boss was generous enough to put me up in his basement. It was a step up from a cold cement jail cell and certainly better than walking the streets in the dead of winter.

One evening, as I wandered downtown in search of my next fix, I felt a sharp pain on my leg. Stooping down, I pulled up my pants and drew in my breath. A huge abscess had developed, infecting my entire leg. I had seen it a few weeks prior but hadn't thought much of it. It had nearly doubled in size since then. Now, beads of sweat were popping out and pricked my forehead, suggesting a sudden fever. I knew I needed help and fast.

***

"Can I help you?" A pleasant nurse met me inside the halls of Good Samaritan Hospital when I stumbled in. She looked me up and down and frowned. I'm sure I must have looked a sight with my unruly hair and rumpled clothes.

"I need help," I said quietly and pulled up my pant leg.

The nurse raised her brow and suddenly gasped. "I'll get you checked in and have a doctor take a look at that right away," she assured me, scurrying away.

JOURNEY TOWARD FREEDOM

A few hours later, the doctor had some grim words for me. "I'll be honest with you, son. You have one of the worst life-threatening abscesses I've ever seen. Your entire body has gone septic. There's a strong chance you'll lose your leg. If you'd come in a day or two later, you could have lost your life."

Delirious from my high fever, I merely nodded and closed my eyes. *Lose your leg ... could have lost your life.* This was serious. To think I'd almost let it go.

Over the next 30 days, I had a total of five surgeries. I was sent to the burn unit to recover, as my right leg had been cut open from my kidney to my knee. My body was also trying to detox from drugs, making my recovery especially painful. It was a horrible, lonely, frightening experience. I refused to contact any friends or family during my hospital stay, not wanting to worry them.

"God, just let me die," I prayed one morning as the doctors wheeled me in for surgery. "Just let me die right there on the operating table. I can't go on like this." I hadn't spoken to God often during my years as a drug addict and wasn't sure he even heard my prayers anymore. What would he want with a strung-out guy who walked the streets in search of his next heroin fix?

As I drifted off to sleep for the surgery, I thought of my wonderful grandmother, who had lived such a vivacious life. She had loved God with her whole heart, right up until the day she died. And she had never given up on me. Was it possible that God hadn't given up on me, either?

I spent the next few weeks propped up in a hospital bed, drifting in and out of sleep with the television blaring in the background. The doctors had a difficult time pumping painkillers into my system, as I had such a high tolerance to drugs. At last, they sent me home with methadone, a substance used to detox the system from drugs. Within days, I was back on the streets, unfazed by my near death experience.

***

With nearly every bridge now burned and no means of making money, I fell into criminal behavior. My life consisted of shooting heroin, walking the streets and shoplifting at Nordstrom and anywhere else I could heist without getting caught. I quickly learned jeans were an easy theft and traded nicely for a needle.

FREEDOM ROAD

The next few months were a nightmarish blur. I moved in and out of detox centers, each time knowing I wasn't ready to truly kick my habit. I contracted Hepatitis C from sharing needles, and shortly after, another large wound showed up on my leg. I went in for yet another surgery, but even that wasn't enough to turn my life around.

Everyone from childhood friends to my grandfather to my probation officer tried to step in, voicing his or her concern for my life.

"I hate to see you like this, Phillip," my friend Stephanie sobbed as she stood over my hospital bed. "You don't have to live like this, you know."

Again, I thought of my grandmother and the snappy little tune, "The B-I-B-L-E." It seemed like a lifetime ago, years separated by pain and hard living. Church, God and the Bible were all good things, but were they enough to save me from my unceasing downhill spiral?

Desperate for help, I called my grandparents (my grandfather was now remarried) who took me in under their roof once again. "There's a place called Freedom House nearby," he told me, his eyes creased with worry. "I want you to go. You have nothing to lose at this point, Phillip."

Skeptical, I shrugged. "What's going to be different this time, Grandpa? You know I've tried to kick this a hundred times. These places are all a joke. You go in, go out and head right back to the streets."

"Please," my grandfather begged. "Just give it a try."

Maybe he's right, I thought reluctantly. What did I have to lose? I was essentially homeless, jobless and had found little success everywhere else I'd gone to try to get clean. I was in trouble with the law and had alienated everyone close to me, including my son. According to several doctors, I was lucky to be alive. How much longer could I keep pushing my luck? I was a desperate man at the end of his rope.

***

The minute I walked into the doors of Freedom House in early January 2008, I knew something was different. People flashed me genuine smiles as they walked down the halls. There were no hardened glances, no judgmental frowns. I could not quite put my finger on it, but I was pretty sure Freedom House was the place I'd been searching for all these empty years.

I met with a wonderful man named Pastor Jim. His eyes were filled with compassion as he spoke to me one morning shortly after I arrived. "We're so glad you are here, Phillip. God cares about you so much. It does not matter where you have been or what you've done. Your past sins can all be forgiven. You simply need to reach out to Jesus. He is the answer and the hope you have been searching for. Won't you give your life to him?"

I didn't have to think twice about my answer. It was as if years of chains had been lifted from my soul. I was ready to surrender. "Yes, I want to. I'm ready." I bowed my head and entered into a simple but life-changing prayer.

"Lord, I know I've done some awful things. But thank you for not giving up on me. I'm tired of this, and I'm done. I need you, because I can't do this anymore on my own."

The minute I opened my eyes, I felt an instant peace wash over me. It was as if the heavens had opened up and Jesus had reached down his hand to touch me. A warmth filled my soul as I smiled for what felt like the first time in years.

Thank you, Lord. Oh, thank you! I knew I had a long road ahead of me, but the wonderful thing was I no longer had to walk it alone.

Freedom House proved to be a safe haven for me, a place where I could not only get clean, but grow in my newfound relationship with the Lord, as well. Instead of "working to pay for my bed" as I'd done in all the other rehab centers, I had time to focus on making genuine, lasting changes in my life. I quickly made friends with my peers and was happily surprised at their genuine warmth toward me. There was no sense of arrogance in anyone. The leaders led a consistent spiritual life and remained committed to helping me grow in my relationship with God, the only thing that could truly bring me healing and freedom.

I had many hours a day to read my Bible and pray. I was amazed at the wonderful passages awaiting me in this little book of treasures. Philippians 4:13 quickly became a favorite verse of mine: "I can do all things through Christ who strengthens me." I also memorized the 23rd Psalm, which brought great comfort to me. I had a good shepherd watching over me. He had not abandoned me when I walked through the "valleys of the shadows of death." Instead, he had simply been waiting for me to find my way back to the green pastures and into his arms.

Each morning, I was amazed at how hungry I was for the word. Instead of pining for my next fix, I found myself yearning for the scriptures. I could not wait to see what the Lord had to say to me that day.

I was also amazed that my filthy language disappeared. For 20 years, I had struggled with a potty mouth, and now, by God's grace, it was gone. As Philippians 4:13 promised, I could do *all* things through Christ. He gave me the strength each day to conquer and move forward in my journey toward healing. I was now a new creature, and all things in my past had been washed away. What a wonderful feeling.

Slowly, my emaciated, sickly frame began to return to a normal, healthy state. The color seeped back into my cheeks, and I began to like who I saw in the mirror each morning. I had experienced not only a spiritual healing, but a physical one, as well.

Life was not all a bed of roses, of course. Years of living a drug-filled life left me struggling to shed my "street mentality." I realized that Satan was engaged in a battle for my soul and that he would love nothing more than to see me fall back into my old ways. Whenever old images or feelings arose, however, I sought out accountability from my peers and leaders in the center. We were on the same team with only one goal in mind: to further our relationship with Jesus Christ.

A few weeks into the program, I began to pray about the past relationships I had struggled with over the years. I asked the Lord to forgive me for my hardened feelings toward Misty and toward my stepmother, who had thrown my belongings out onto the porch that one summer morning. God also put it on my heart to reconcile with my biological father.

"I know it's been a long time, Dad, but I'm a new person now," I told him with a quivering voice when we spoke at last. "I want to ask for your forgiveness and let you know I've forgiven you, as well. I have found a wonderful relationship with God, and it is through him that I am able to put my past behind me. I would love to get to know you again."

To my surprise and relief, my father was receptive to my heartfelt words.

JOURNEY TOWARD FREEDOM

"Thank you, Phillip. It's so wonderful to hear you say that. I never stopped thinking about you after all these years."

I restored my relationship with my grandparents, as well. They were elated that I had taken their advice to come to Freedom House. These two people, Grandpa Jim and Grandma Joyce, literally stepped in the gap to help save me from myself. The godly compassion and longsuffering they extended made a real impact on me, especially Grandma Joyce, who, when she married my grandpa, didn't know she was signing up for this!

Grandpa told me one day, "I'm going to send you a letter I wrote just before you entered the program. In the letter, I cried out to God, asking him to please save you and help you turn your life around. He heard my desperate prayers, Phillip. I never gave up on you, and neither did God."

Joy filled my soul as I thanked the Lord for his faithfulness. Knowing my grandfather had been praying for me during all those years meant the world to me. I knew it was no mistake that I came to Freedom House. The only explanation for my genuine change of heart was God's amazing timing and healing. He had been preparing me for this place even when I hadn't a clue what my life held next. It had taken hitting rock bottom for me to surrender to him. I knew there would be no turning back now.

"It's easy to see now why this place is called Freedom House," I chuckled to Pastor Jim one day. "I never thought I'd experience true freedom from my life of addiction. I tried so many times, but I could never quite get there. I now see it's because I hadn't found the true source of hope and healing: Jesus."

That night, as I slipped into bed, I pulled out my Bible and ran my fingers over the leather cover. Now singing in heaven, my grandmother's little song to me when I was young popped into my head once again. "The B-I-B-L-E, yes, that's the book for me ..." All those years ago, Grandma had had it right. All of life's answers are wrapped up in God's word.

***

As I reflect now over so much pain and loss in the past, I have to give praise to my Lord and Savior, Jesus Christ. He is helping me to grow strong in faith and walk out this newfound freedom within. I have seen his favor helping me with the criminal justice system, I have been able to find the grace to handle some of the most painful memories of my past and he's freed me from more than two decades of life as a dope fiend. The Lord rejoices to restore what the enemy has taken. I hope and pray to be a godly influence in my son, Tyler's, life one day. He deserves so much more than I have been to him.

As I flip the Bible open to see what God has in store for me tonight, I wonder if Grandma is looking down on me right now, smiling.

"You've got it, son!" I can almost hear her say. "You've got it at last!" And with that thought, I smile.

"I got it, Grandma. I got it."

SPARED
The Story of Derick Tungwenuk
Written by Ellen R. Hale

Emergency room doctors and nurses stared down at me in disbelief.

"Oh my God."

"Angel in heaven."

"Holy cow."

I searched the faces of the growing crowd that was suddenly and inexplicably fascinated with me. Most were shaking their heads.

"What's wrong with me?" I finally dared to ask.

As they returned to their patients one by one, the surprising answers came.

"You're fine."

"You are one lucky boy."

"It's just ... I've never seen anything like that before."

The car accident replayed in my mind. My friends and I had hopped in two cars and raced down the streets of Portland to grab sandwiches at Subway. I smoked pot in the passenger seat while my friend, who was eight months pregnant, drove another friend's car. No need for seatbelts.

In one long moment, my friend sped up to dart in front of the other car. Striking a manhole, she overcorrected, and we skidded across four lanes of traffic. I looked over at my friends in the other car and saw their eyes grow wide at the impending collision.

Crash! I heard glass shattering and the horrible sound of steel buckling all around me.

When I opened my eyes, the car had bounced several feet back from the 4-foot square pillar of brick. I turned toward my pregnant friend. The driver's seat was empty. Frantically, I struggled to open the passenger door as my eyes darted through the gaping hole where the windshield once was.

"Where's my friend?" I asked, a bit more calmly as I surveyed the wreckage.

"She's fine. She's right over there," I heard people tell me.

"My friend! Is she okay? I can't see her!"

"You need to sit down," someone gently suggested.

"I'm fine! I'm fine! I've gotta find …"

"Look at your arm, son."

Bone was visible for all to see on my left arm. My flesh had been sliced through and peeled away on impact, exposing the pulsing veins. My head suddenly felt like a watermelon about to burst. I tasted blood in my mouth. Sitting down, I saw that my shirt was dripping in blood. I put my hand to my face, and tiny pieces of glass poked my fingers.

"I need a cigarette," I said wearily, slumping down to sit on the ground.

The sound of sirens neared as a firefighter flicked the cigarette out of my hand.

"You don't need that right now," he snapped.

They hurried me into an ambulance and rushed me to the emergency room, where the staff spent two hours stitching up my lacerated arm. A nurse who was picking the shards of glass out of my hair and face asked me what happened.

I told her everything I remembered.

"I think my friend leaned over me as we crashed to protect her baby, and she flew out the windshield," I said, recalling the ordeal.

"It's amazing you're still alive," the nurse said, cleaning dried blood off my ear and neck. "Okay, turn your head to the left."

She gasped in such a way that it drew a crowd in the ER.

There was another deep cut that stretched across almost the entire right side of my neck. The cut stopped on either side of my jugular vein, which carries blood from the head to the heart. If that vein would have been severed, I would have died within minutes.

God had spared my life again. But I couldn't be as enthusiastic as the medical professionals who marveled at the miracle. *Thank you, Lord. I guess. That would have been a really good time to take me. Why didn't you? I wish I were dead.*

When my arm healed, scars remained. One scar actually formed a cross.

***

My sister, Dana, and I cried together on the living room couch. Our father had come home drunk — again — and my mom hurriedly prepared us to leave. Dana consoled me as they argued, trying to help me get my arm through the sleeve of my shirt when our mother hit the floor.

Dad gripped her wrists tightly and held her down.

"I won't let you leave me!" he hollered in her face.

We didn't leave that night, but eventually my parents split up. Dana was 5 years old, and I was 4. The summer after their divorce, I stayed with my maternal grandparents on their farm in Myrtle Point. Mom was busy back in Portland attending school and working.

My uncle Stacey lived on the farm, too, attending high school at the time. He was born when my mom was 18, so he was like a big brother to me. We spent the days caring for the cows and pigs, feeding the ducks and fishing and hiking in the woods. We also drew water from a well.

Down by the well was a hillside Stacey loved jumping down. One day, he urged me to try this jump, and I wanted to impress him, maybe even jumping farther than he could. I gathered all my strength and started running, giving a mighty heave, but rather than make it, I somehow lost my balance and landed on my back with a huge thud. Suddenly, I couldn't breathe. There I was, staring up at the blue sky and fast-moving clouds, tasting sand in my mouth. I still couldn't breathe. Was I going to die?

"Are you okay?" Stacey laughed, pulling me up on my feet. "Looks like you got the wind knocked out of you."

Dana was the always-obedient daughter, while I misbehaved constantly. For some reason, I was obsessed with fire. My mom smoked cigarettes, and I loved to steal them, play with her lighter and mimic her smoking.

One day, Mom was taking a bath, so I grabbed one of her lighters and sneaked under her bed. Suddenly, a flame ignited the bottom of the bed. When Mom smelled smoke, she emerged from the bathroom naked, flipped the mattress against the wall, started scooping her bathwater with a plastic tub and dumped scoop after scoop on the fire.

That disaster — and my mom hiding her lighters from me — still didn't deter me from continuing to play with fire. Next to our yellow house was a small sheep pasture. One day, we discovered a smoldering burn pile in that pasture that looked as if it was about to go out. I ran back in the house while my mom was napping and lit some newspapers on our stove, determined to help get the burn pile going again. Dana coached me in safety most of the time, but she also helped me get it going and do it right at times, too.

I remember I lit a page of newspaper on the stove to take to the burn pile, but the flame always died out before I'd reach the now dying embers of the burn pile. As I arrived back at the smoldering spot in the field, Dana advised me not to run.

"Take bigger steps instead. Then maybe the newspaper will stay lit."

Besides being both a protector and encourager, my sister also filled the roles of companion, caretaker and instructor. But despite her best efforts, she couldn't stop me from screwing up. We were strapped in the backseat of the car Mom had just rented after an accident when she realized she forgot something inside the house. Wanting to drive like my mom, I climbed into the front seat and started moving the gearshift lever.

"What are you doing, Derick?" Dana asked. "You're supposed to stay back here."

No sooner had the words left her mouth than I accidentally pushed the gear into neutral. Slowly, the car began rolling downhill toward the largest tree in our yard. Panicking, I tried to steer, but we kept heading straight. The collision broke the bumper of the rental car, but thankfully, we were unharmed. Needless to say, my mom was very angry.

Once Dana learned to ride her bike, she decided to teach me. She put the training wheels back on her bike and let me ride. When she felt that I was ready, she removed the training wheels and guided me as I began pedaling on my own.

Eventually, she knew she could let me go and I'd glide down the driveway all by myself.

***

The playroom was filled with crayons and coloring books, toys, board games and movies. Everything I could want — except someone to play with. My mom never left my sister's hospital bed down the hall. Like Dana, all the other kids who were in the hospital were too sick to play.

I didn't understand hospitals. Why did we have to come here so often? And weren't doctors supposed to make people feel better? Yet Dana came home from the hospital sicker than when she arrived. Her illness was heavy on my heart, and I would often slip down to the hospital chapel and ask God to heal her.

When Dana was 9 years old, they told me she had a cancer called leukemia and needed chemotherapy treatments, which made her extremely weak. When her beautiful straight black hair began falling out, she tied a bandanna around her head, and we headed into school together, only to be greeted by kids who teased her.

The chemo failed to stop the cancer, and Dana developed a starfish-shaped growth on the back of her head. She underwent surgery to remove the brain tumor, but doctors were unsuccessful because it was too big. Soon, Dana was confined to a hospital bed in our home. I walked to school by myself and quickly plummeted from a straight-A student to a straight-F student. Jealousy consumed me as I watched Dana stay up late watching television while I had to go to bed and spend the whole day at school. *Talk about special treatment.*

My mom, Dana and I had started attending a Baptist church, and members of the congregation overwhelmed us with love and support. They brought our family meals, and everyone was praying for Dana. I heard Bible stories in Sunday school and learned how to pray. I was certain God would heal my sister. After all, she deserved to live — she was the good girl who always followed the rules. Dana and I *had* to get back to frolicking in our aboveground pool, climbing on playground equipment and hiding inside the long branches of the weeping willow tree in our yard.

The phone rang in the middle of the night one weekend while I was staying with my dad and stepmother at their home in Vancouver.

A few minutes later, my dad opened the door and collapsed on my bed.

"Dana just died," he choked out before he began sobbing.

Tears welled up in my eyes, but I didn't cry. *What is wrong with me?* I wondered.

At the funeral in our Baptist church, I sat stoically in the wooden pew. Everyone else was weeping over the loss of my sister, grieved over a young life snuffed out and for the gaping hole left in my family.

But I didn't cry.

JOURNEY TOWARD FREEDOM

***

After Dana died, everyone assumed I couldn't handle it. My school allowed me to pass third grade even though I flunked. My mom bought me a dog — a Dalmatian mutt — that I named Tom, simply because I didn't have any friends named Tom.

My dog replaced my sister in many ways. Tom and I would tramp into the woods, where I'd start fires and he'd dig furiously to put them out. Tom would come when I called and jump around happily when I practiced my karate moves.

One winter day, the streets were slick with snow and another dog was making his way across the street. Suddenly, I saw a car careening toward him, horn blaring and wheels locked. That man hit that dog, and I found myself thinking, *That dog dying is my fault.* The incident made me both sad and angry at the same time. I burst into tears and then marveled that I could cry over a dog and not cry about my sister.

In the fall, my mom enrolled me in Christian school and made appointments for me to visit a psychiatrist. Little did she know I had already shut down emotionally.

There's nothing you can do about it, I thought as I visited with the psychiatrist during my first appointment. I would tell him whatever I thought he wanted to hear, but when the time came, I said to him, "I don't want to talk about her."

The psychiatrist, a well-groomed middle-aged man, convinced me that my problem was rooted in my inability to relax. On subsequent visits, he instructed me to close my eyes and relax each part of my body from my toes to my head. He then asked me where I had difficulty relaxing my body. I told him my stomach.

"So, you're relaxed here?" he asked, placing his hand on my groin.

And with that, I was victimized again. He told me that our relaxation work was between him and me.

"Don't tell your parents about it," he warned.

***

My first experience with sexual abuse had occurred soon after my parents divorced. Dana and I shared a room on the second floor of our house. Our beds were on opposite sides of the room, with a window and two dressers between them. A calendar hung on the wall with a list of chores that we would mark off.

A teenage daughter of my mom's friend began to babysit us. She brought us up the creaking stairs to our bedroom, where she told Dana to stay on her bed. Dana was *so* obedient. Meanwhile, the babysitter took off my clothes and began rubbing her body against mine. I looked over at Dana in desperation as the babysitter expressed her pleasure out loud. Dana was trying not to watch. *Why won't you help me?!*

"Stay there," the babysitter ordered Dana. "You two will get in big trouble if you tell anyone about this."

By the time I began sleeping over at the home of a friend from the Christian school, I knew to keep my mouth shut when his stepfather snuck in late at night to fondle us while he thought we were sleeping. It was just another horrible moment that I had to endure alone.

***

Two particular families at church were extraordinarily kind to me, including our pastor's family. After Sunday services, I frequently spent time with the families. We cooked barbecues and went bowling.

I sincerely believed what I learned at church: that God sent Jesus to die and give me forgiveness of my sins. On camping trips, I told other kids about Jesus and urged them to pray and ask the Lord for their salvation, or go talk to my mom.

Eventually, I began talking to my pastor about baptism. Everything he explained about baptism being a "new birth" sounded great to me. I wanted a new life because I couldn't remember a time when I was innocent. I was constantly in trouble at the Christian school, forced to stay inside and complete homework while my classmates played outside. My parents were divorced, and my sister was dead — instead of me. I was convinced baptism would erase my painful past.

But when my pastor dunked me under the water and pulled me up again, I didn't feel reborn at all. Disappointment washed over me instead. *I'm the same. That didn't work at all.*

The only time I found peace was during the summer nights, when I'd sneak out of the house and ride my bike wherever I pleased. The rest of the time I felt like a stubborn lone bowling pin about to be knocked down again.

Leaving school and taking a long bike ride one early summer afternoon, I came home and jumped in the shower. Suddenly, all the bottled-up emotions poured out of me. I felt as though I was breathing in sorrow instead of steam as the feelings over losing my perfect sister broke my heart. For some reason, I thought about Uncle Stacey with deep sadness, too. I dropped to my knees and cried like I never had before.

After drying off and dressing, I became annoyed. *I'm trying to forget my sister.*

That better not happen again.

I fell asleep in the TV room that night and awoke to the loud ring of the telephone. My mom was a sound sleeper and didn't answer. The phone kept ringing, over and over again. I finally heard my mom's muffled voice.

"No, no," she wailed into the phone. "Not Stacey, too?"

I heard my mom's knees hit the floor as she stumbled into the TV room. She was gasping for air and grabbed hold of me. I knew inside that Stacey had died.

My grandmother had called to share the awful news — Stacey, who was now in college, was killed in a drunk driving accident that afternoon.

I tried to hold up my mother and comfort her.

"I know, I know." My words sounded hollow. Inside, my anger toward God rose up. *Why him and not me? He was a good guy, and I'm rebellious to the core.*

Embittered, I reasoned that this was how life was. I had no choice but to accept it and move on. At Stacey's graveside, I was asking God why I couldn't cry, first for my sister or my uncle Stacey. I felt bad over their passing, but there just weren't any tears.

***

In seventh grade, I returned to public school. I finally found a best friend who understood me and my sense of humor. Dave and Derick — people couldn't seem to say one name without the other.

At Dave's house, liquor was readily available. We mixed our own screwdrivers and began to crave how liberated drinking made us feel.

SPARED

During freshman year, we began our school day by drinking in the dugout of the baseball field. We'd be drunk through half the day, then drink again when we arrived home from school. My girlfriend's parents were potheads, so she always had access to marijuana. Soon we joined her in smoking.

We got completely wasted before the homecoming football game. As the floats traveled around the track, a spectacle unfolded: Dave was on a float, mooning the crowd. The principal intervened, and when she found me, she could tell I was drunk, too. We were swiftly suspended.

Sophomore year brought new highs as we experimented with other drugs: mushrooms, LSD, cocaine. Although I had been taught drugs were bad, the peer pressure was too strong. I needed my friends to continue accepting me. And I needed the escape.

That school year, I was caught drinking again and was ordered to attend alternative school for three months. It was my second treatment program. I graduated and returned to school, but when my mom found me drinking again, she sent me away to an inpatient program. I lasted there 16 days before our insurance money ran out. I thought I was getting the boot because no one could tell me what to do; nothing would change my rebellious ways.

Dave was a year older than me, so when he obtained his driver's license, we were instantly "cool." A three-car caravan of guys, including Dave and me, drove out to the coast for a fishing trip. All of us had been drinking when my driver lost control around a curve. We slammed into a truck parked on the side of the road. Fortunately, no one was seriously hurt, but the truck owner was injured in the spin. I suffered a concussion but didn't tell anyone. Had it not been for the truck, we would have plunged into the swollen Nestucca River and likely died.

The accident failed to serve as a wakeup call, and I continued to party. My senior year, school officials discovered me with marijuana and a pipe with cocaine residue. They had no other recourse than to expel me — a month and a half before graduation. I had become the failure I always knew I was.

Even though I hadn't been to church since age 14, one of my friends from church still lived in the neighborhood. After my expulsion, this childhood friend suggested I apply to work at Round Table Pizzeria with her. At first, all I would do was take pizza orders over the phone. But whenever co-workers needed someone to take their shifts, I jumped at the opportunity. I thrived on working hard and making money. However, it wasn't all business, as one night a co-worker and I stole a keg of beer.

Before long, the manager gave me a supervisory role. I gained the responsibility of locking up the restaurant at night, which fed my desire to be in control. I spent six years working at Round Table, eventually earning a promotion to assistant manager of another restaurant in the chain.

My drug use kept growing as did my income during this time. Although I lived at home with Mom, I spent almost every night in my girlfriend's apartment.

High school friends who I frequently got high with also lived downstairs. So in the morning, my girlfriend would head to school, and I'd head to work.

One night, I changed my comfortable routine and didn't stop at my friends' place for alcohol and drugs. As we slept that night, the smoke detector in my girlfriend's apartment shocked me awake in the darkness. Wisps of smoke floated toward the ceiling. I sprinted to the front door, and when I opened it, a huge wall of black smoke instantly engulfed me. I slammed the door shut realizing in that moment that we were on the second floor.

My girlfriend was sound asleep, oblivious to the raging fire.

"Wake up! Wake up!" I yelled, shaking her.

"What?" she said sleepily. Then she smelled the smoke.

"Get your clothes on! We've gotta go out the window!" I calmly began to formulate a plan. "I'll tie a sheet around you and lower you down."

She yanked the screen out and pushed the window open. I ripped the sheet off our bed and started tying a knot.

"The ladder!" my girlfriend suddenly remembered.

I had forgotten — her father had insisted on the smoke detector and ladder in case there was a fire. At the time, I dismissed the precautions as coming from an overprotective father, but now we were extremely grateful for his care.

After escaping the apartment, we used the ladder to help other residents escape the four-alarm blaze. One lady died. We found out the fire started in my friends' apartment when a newspaper had fallen on the baseboard heater.

I had been playing with fire my entire life, and finally flames had nearly consumed me.

SPARED

Because I didn't drink or do drugs until I passed out this particular night, my girlfriend and I were unharmed by the fire.

I evaded death once again — for at least the fifth time in my young life.

My girlfriend and I celebrated our good fortune by moving in together. I finally had it all — a great job, a great car and a great girl to spend the rest of my life with. Surely my excessive drinking wouldn't do any harm.

Or so I thought. After I was arrested for Driving Under the Influence (DUI) more than once, my girlfriend demanded I quit. I made promise after promise to her and quickly broke them. We had been together for three years when she left me.

That gave me permission to plunge into a drinking free-for-all. When Round Table fired me, I had lost everything I prized.

I moved to a studio apartment in northwest Portland and found minimum-wage work at an oxidizing company, the family business of a friend from high school. Despondent that I had lost my career in restaurant management and the love of my life, it wasn't long before I arrived at work late or didn't bother going at all. When they fired me, I became a full-blown alcoholic. Any money I made I spent on liquor instead of bills. The utility company shut off my heat, and my landlord threatened to evict me. I ate only a few times a week. Thoughts of suicide flooded my mind, and I actually made a few feeble attempts to take my own life.

Each of my parents did what they could to help me financially for a while before they realized they had to stop enabling me. Continuing down the path that started when I sipped my first screwdriver as a teenager, I told Satan that I would be his as long as he kept me drunk. *I just want to be drunk the rest of my life.*

Desperate for fast cash, I donated my plasma and headed straight to the liquor store to buy vodka.

If God refused to take my life, it was about time I did.

***

The smell of the ashtray reminded me I wanted a cigarette as soon as I woke up. Slowly opening my eyes, the sight of a bloody razor startled my intoxicated mind. Then I remembered. I rolled over and stood up, making the room spin. The stain of blood on the floor made me feel like I was about to vomit.

JOURNEY TOWARD FREEDOM

I had been staring into the bathroom mirror the night before. *Look at you. You're pathetic. Why don't you just kill yourself?* I grabbed a plastic razor without thinking, but I was simply too drunk to even get it out of the package or separate the blade from the mount. Returning to my room, I flipped on the TV and smoked a cigarette. *You might as well do it. Just slice your wrist and lie down in bed. You'll pass out and die in your sleep.*

Now, I couldn't believe my eyes. My wrist bore a cut, but it wasn't bleeding. For a moment, I thanked God that he spared me once again. Then my deep-seated anger and bitterness overtook me. *I can't even kill myself right.*

One day, I was biking over to cash a tax return check and drink the money away. I thought I would stay in a hotel or something if I got too messed up.

While wheeling along an overpass over the freeway, my front wheel came off, and I was falling into the blackness. I found myself in the middle of the highway in a life-threatening situation. Even at that moment, there were no cars around, and all I ended up needing was stitches in my face.

Here was yet another death-defying moment to ponder.

***

Life became a predictable cycle after my suicide attempt — short-lived jobs, short-lived relationships, short-lived stints in treatment programs. No quick fixes worked. I racked up more DUIs and FTAs — Failure To Appear — in court.

I was living with another co-dependent, and our constant arguments sometimes drove me to spend the night in a hotel. On one such occasion, I picked up the phone in the hotel room and called my girlfriend. "I'm going to kill myself," I said flatly.

"Can I call you right back?" she responded.

I slammed the phone down and returned to my beer and marijuana. *She doesn't care about me at all.*

Several minutes later, there was a knock on my door. It was the police. The phone rang.

"You called the police, didn't you?" I growled at my girlfriend.

"I didn't know what else to do."

"No, you did the right thing," I sighed, letting the officers inside.

SPARED

Once they discovered my outstanding warrants, they arrested me. I spent six months in jail. Amazingly, my girlfriend and I stayed together. But once I was released, I reverted to the same lifestyle. One night, I drove her car to several bars and was arrested for DUI for the fourth time in 10 years.

After three days in jail, my court-appointed attorney told me to expect a seven-year prison sentence. Knowing my freedom was gone, my heart sank and my soul stirred. Back in my cell, I fell to my knees and cried.

"Lord, I can't do this anymore," I admitted. "I need you."

I confessed to God everything I had done wrong and everything I was angry about — my parents' divorce, my sister's death, my uncle's death, the sexual abuse. All the emotions I conditioned myself to bury deep inside erupted. As suddenly as the tears came, they stopped. A few minutes of silence passed before I smiled and laughed.

Inside the 5-foot-by-6-foot cell, I was imprisoned. But inside my heart, for the first time in my life, I was free. God took away my physical freedom to show me spiritual freedom. He wanted all of my attention, and now he had it.

You're alive for a reason, Derick. I won't let you die because I have a plan for your future.

***

The lack of distractions in jail allowed me to easily embrace my rediscovered faith. I prayed constantly and read the Bible a lot. At first, my prayers focused on God's will to be done in my court case.

My attorney argued that certain DUI charges shouldn't count because of the time or place they occurred. Grudgingly, the judge admitted that the attorney was right and sentenced me to only 20 months.

Once in prison, I heard a sermon on the radio in my cell that really spoke to me. *Lord, I'd really like to meet this preacher someday. Maybe I could even go to his church.* It was a short, simple prayer.

As my release date neared, I began to pray that God would provide me with a church, a job and a place to live. Also on my heart were two people from my past — Rachelle, the girlfriend I thought I would marry, and Mark, an old friend of mine from church life.

My mom told me her friend, who I called Aunt Sheila, agreed to let me move into her home. Her stepson worked at Newport Bay (the same restaurant which I was working at when my prison stretch called me away), and it was likely I could return to the restaurant business as a cook at a different location. God was answering my prayers!

I was transferred back to jail before my release, and now I only needed a way to get to Aunt Sheila's home in Beaverton since my parents were both out of town. Overhearing another inmate's conversation, I discovered he had the same release date and was heading home to Beaverton with his mother. They had no problem giving me a ride.

God had done so much for me that I didn't deserve! I was determined to keep following him. I found out there was a church within walking distance of Aunt Sheila's home. When I slept in my first Sunday morning out of jail, I felt incredibly guilty. I set out to find the church, and it turned out I couldn't miss Southwest Bible Church. Attending a large church? I wasn't sure. Then I saw that a 6 p.m. service was scheduled for Sunday night.

I raced home to eat and to read my Bible. Not wanting to miss the start of the service, I headed back to the church at 4:30. While I waited, I made myself comfortable in the coffee shop. A man soon joined me and invited me to sit with his family during the service.

I grabbed the visitor's card and wrote down my contact information. Would I like information about the church? Check. About the men's ministry? Check. About the singles' ministry? Check. About missions? Check. While I focused on my card, the pastor walked on stage.

"Welcome, friends," he began.

I stopped scribbling as tears filled my eyes. The voice belonged to the pastor I had listened to on the radio in prison. God had brought me to the church where I belonged.

During my first day at work, I heard another familiar voice. There walking past the restaurant pass thru window in a server's uniform was my ex-girlfriend.

"Rachelle?" I called out.

She was as shocked to see me as I was to see her. I approached her as she was counting her tips at the end of her shift.

SPARED

"How are you doing? How's your family?" We spent several minutes catching up. A weight lifted off me when I learned she was doing well.

"Do you remember my friend, Jenny?" she asked.

"Yeah, of course."

"You won't believe this, but she's married to Mark Williams."

"No way!"

The realization that God had shown me the answers to all my prison-cell prayers in one week gave me goose bumps.

I believe, Lord. I believe.

***

The management at Newport Bay knew there was one condition to my employment — no working Sundays. Inevitably, the restaurant ended up short-staffed, and the co-worker I was now living with asked me to cover a Sunday shift.

"No, I can't," I told him. "I'm putting God first. It's the first day of the week, and I'm going to church."

"It kills me to ask you, Derick," he said. "I know how good you're doing. But please, just cover this next Sunday. Then I'll fix the schedule so it doesn't happen again."

"I won't come in until noon, though. Then I can go to church in the morning."

When I wasn't an alcoholic, I was a workaholic. Soon one Sunday shift turned into every Sunday. I rationalized the compromise by telling myself I could always go to the Wednesday service. But being on the night schedule had me staying up later and waking up later. I started slipping away from my church attendance and involvement.

Temptation lurked during my ride home from work — as one local bar stood out, beckoning me to come inside. I finally gave in. Sitting down at the bar, I remembered fun times with old friends. The arcade games beeped and pinged in my ears with creepy electronic voices boasting "play me!" and "give it a try!"

The bartender fixed me a rum and coke, and the smooth glass slid into my hand. The smell of smoke and alcohol was detestable. Stirring my drink and staring at the dark, bubbly liquid, I knew I should walk away.

Just drink it. You know you want it.

JOURNEY TOWARD FREEDOM

In one swift move, I took the first drink and thought, *There, that's over. Now I can drink like a gentleman.* I drank that glass and ordered another. Then I left.

Wow, I did it. I had two drinks and didn't get drunk. No big deal.

I should have known better. Very quickly, I lost my job and home as alcoholism took over my life again. I tried, with little success, various inpatient treatment programs, halfway houses, AA meetings and the Salvation Army's Adult Rehabilitation Center. On the second try, I graduated from the Salvation Army program, and my mom and stepfather allowed me to housesit while they were out of town for two weeks.

To celebrate New Year's 2007, I drove my mom's car to the nearest bar. As I prepared to leave, I double-parked her car while I emptied the car of beer bottles. Drawing the attention of a police officer, I was in the hot seat again. However, because the keys weren't in the ignition, he couldn't charge me with another DUI. Nevertheless, I had just gotten off post-prison supervision, so obviously it was a heavy hit to now have a new violation and thus end up right back in jail.

Relief began to fill my soul since I knew that being inside again would mean being protected from myself. In fact, I actually anticipated experiencing spiritual freedom and closeness to God again.

Every week, members of Evergreen Christian Center came to the jail to take inmates to church. I jumped at the opportunity. I was eligible for a work-release program and obtained my best job yet as an exhibition cook in the cafeteria at Oregon Health & Science University. After my release, I quickly connected with a student who needed a roommate.

Two weeks passed, and I was drinking again. Daily. My roommate returned my deposit and ordered me to find another place to live. When I lingered before moving, he started staying elsewhere.

***

Drunk and alone in the apartment, I stared blankly at the TV when a program called *Crystal Darkness* about methamphetamine addiction caught my attention. A help number popped up on the screen, and I dialed it.

"Is this just for people with meth problems?" I asked the operator. "Because I'm a 31-year-old alcoholic."

The operator suggested AA.

"I know about AA," I explained. "I've been doing that for years."

"Have you ever heard of Freedom House?"

Freedom House? That sounds like what I need.

I took the phone number and left a message for the staff. When I learned that Freedom House was a yearlong program, I hesitated. A year was way too long to be in treatment! Still, all other options had run out.

I made an appointment for an interview with Freedom House's founder, Pastor Jim. In his office, I settled into a comfortable chair and noticed his family photos and Bible verses decorating the room. Multiple Bibles, well used and dust free, lay around the room.

For the first time, I told the truth about my alcoholism and my long-buried emotions. From the time my sister died, I had been telling people what they wanted to hear so they would leave me alone. At other treatment programs, I knew what I needed to say to get in and get it over with. I was never honest.

Pastor Jim showed me the schedule, and I was impressed with its structure. He handed me the story of a Freedom House graduate to read and left the room.

"Lord," I prayed, "if you want me here, I want to be here."

So I got sober and enrolled on October 28.

***

"If you hold to my teaching, you are really my disciples," Jesus declared in John 8:31-32. "Then you will know the truth, and the truth will set you free."

I am learning the truth about myself day after day at Freedom House. Many character flaws — selfishness, pride, anger, bitterness — have been exposed to my previously unseeing eyes. The structure at Freedom House is making me disciplined about my faith, to the point where I delight in a disciplined lifestyle.

No other treatment program has given me the intimacy and accountability I need to conquer alcoholism. When I behave in ways that displease God, I don't justify them anymore. Taking responsibility for my wrongs and experiencing restoration has helped me regain a spirit of innocence, a sense of cleanness within.

Most of all, life is no longer about me. It's about what God is doing and what I can do for him. When I was making money in the restaurant business, cleanliness was a top priority. Now that I'm working for God, how much more effort should I put into even simple tasks like completing the daily chores in my room? I pray that he uses me as a leader in the future, but for now, I need to learn to consistently follow him.

***

At Christmas, the Freedom House residents assisted the Eastside Foursquare Church with a dinner theater. Here I was back to doing what I knew best — serving meals — but everything was different. We set up for the performances, prayed for the audience members, served them dinner during the play, tore down afterward and rejoiced over how many people decided to accept Christ as their Savior.

The Other Wise Man is the story of a fourth wise man who saw the Christmas star and sold all his possessions to buy three precious jewels for the baby Jesus. Because he encountered a dying man and nursed him back to health, he missed leaving for Bethlehem with the other wise men. By the time he arrived, the king had ordered the killing of all boys 2 years and younger. Confronted by a soldier, the fourth wise man had the courage to protect a woman's child from death.

As I thought about the message of that drama, I began to see myself in it. I realized that I was that child who, countless times, was so mercifully spared from death because of the protection of my all-wise and loving Savior. Today, I no longer question why it was that I lived or survived. Instead, I carefully consider how God wants me to live. Today, with a heart that is clean and a soul that is enjoying spiritual freedom within, I realize my life is truly a life worth living.

A CRY TO BELONG
The Story of Nick
Written by Diane Popenhagen

It's weird, you know, how loneliness can creep into your soul before you even know you have one. I think I was born lonely. I don't ever remember becoming isolated, so I must have been born not just alone, but a loner. The need to belong is an aching drive that steers itself sometimes and drives too fast around the turns and always tries to race the trains.

This need steered me outside to the smoking section of the schoolyard. I was about 15 years old. Maybe, just maybe, I could fit in with the smokers and class-ditchers. Like a band-aid on a severed limb, smoking with those guys might somehow cover the gaping wound that kept me awake at night.

The wet blacktop shone as I made my way to the "smokers' tree." The smokers were all crowded together in a convoluted circle, like refugees huddling for safety in a place far from home. I watched my nervous steps, with my fists shoved deep into the pockets of my ripped jeans. I stood outside the circle, wiped my rebellious hair from my face and choked out, "Dude, can I bum a smoke?"

Did that sound realistic enough to convince them? I'll never know. Someone gave me a cigarette, either way. He lit it, and I tried not to cough like the geeks I saw on the anti-smoking commercials on TV. I felt like my brain was lighter than the rest of my body and a little like I was going to puke. I continued to trace the outline of my worn shoes with my eyes. I could feel their stares judging me, considering the gamble of friendship. Was I a safe bet? Were they?

I turned to walk back to the school building with the nauseating taste of cigarettes lingering in my dry, nervous mouth. My steps on the freshly polished tile floor echoed in the already-empty hall. I looked up to see the water fountain, like an oasis, offering a break from the taste that had invaded my mouth. The cool water washed every hint of the cigarette away, so I swallowed deep and savored long.

JOURNEY TOWARD FREEDOM

When I entered the room late and all eyes followed my every move, my teacher watched me with suspicion.

She accused, "You're late. You don't have a pass. Do you have an excuse?"

Without lifting up my gaze, I mumbled, "Just give me the stinking tardy."

"What did you just say? Nick, you just bought yourself a one-way pass to detention. Go to the office," the exasperated teacher ordered.

The hall was just as shiny and just as empty going to the office as it was going to class.

But nothing could steal the hope that I could eventually belong with the guys I smoked with that day. I had a chance to be part of something. That was worth the detention.

***

Alone in my bedroom, the isolation seemed insurmountable. When I searched the vocabulary in my adolescent mind to express my sadness, I would simply groan. In my dreams, I would watch the useless words fall on the ground and shatter like glass. I was trapped inside my own anguish.

Cold sweat dampened my palm as I gripped the razor blade in my quivering hands. My ribs threatened to give way under the pounding of my heart. In my solitude, I lifted the blade high and cut deep into my thigh. The searing pain paled next to the ache in my soul. My lips never even cried out. Blood soaked my jeans when I removed the blade.

I ran the sharp edge along my forearm to watch more of the pain trickle into streams of release onto my shower floor. Pools of crimson captured my focus. Self-mutilation may be a mystery to some, but when you are hurting so greatly inside, cutting yourself is one level of pain you can feel in control about.

Later, my father's tall frame stood above me. Before I even knew it, he had entered my room.

"Nick, what's going on in here?" my dad asked as he noticed the cuts.

"I don't know, Dad. I don't even know," I replied, still numb.

My parents' continuous search for outside intervention began that day. It started with the school psychologist and ended with a psychiatrist who simply couldn't reach far enough to touch where I was hurting. I eventually quit cutting my skin, but my soul was still torn to pieces.

***

My tennis shoes sank in the saturated ground on my path to the smoking circle. I raised my gaze just long enough to see a big grin on my buddy's face. His surplus army gear and long hair had become more comforting than my own mom. He was cool. He was who I wanted to be.

He shoved his fists deep into the pockets of his camouflaged pants. "Hey, Nick. Wanna try some weed? It sure makes classes less of a drag," Matt offered.

"Sure. I never tried it. Will I even be okay enough to go back to class?" I asked in obvious naiveté.

"Yeah, you'll enjoy the classes, instead of sleeping," he laughed.

"All right, give it to me. Do I smoke it like a cigarette?" I inquired.

Had it not been an addict giving another teen boy drugs, Matt's patient instruction and tips on smoking weed would have been considered kind tutoring. He was even nice enough to cover me in his dad's cologne. I guess we figured that smelling like an old, fat dad was much better than smelling like weed.

The pot burned all the way down my throat, and my lungs felt too full to hold it all. The snapping sounds from unnoticed seeds were so much different than smoking cigarettes, but marijuana sure tasted better.

"See? What did I tell you? You ready to go back to class now? At least it'll be interesting for a change," Matt assured as he walked beside me to the door.

The same shiny floors and neglected lockers greeted my floating brain, but my legs seemed to hum this time as I strolled back to class. I sat heavy in my chair. My arms lay still on my desk to defy the very real sensation that they were vibrating. The teacher looked at me in scorn, as did most of the students. This time, I was too high to care what they thought.

Pot didn't make me belong. It made me numb to the painful exclusion residing in my chest.

JOURNEY TOWARD FREEDOM

***

I sat nervously in one of the three chairs facing the principal's desk. I studied the degrees and certificates on the wall as if I hadn't seen them every day. I ran my fingers over the smooth wooden desk waiting for Principal Jacobs to return. His gruff voice and angry red face didn't even make my heart beat faster anymore.

I heard the door creak open. I stayed facing the office chair behind the desk, not caring enough to even turn around. As my eyes turned away from the chair to rest on the hole in the left knee of my jeans, two people came in and sat on either side of me. I knew by the shoes I saw that the people were my parents.

"What are you guys doing here?" I asked.

"Principal Jacobs called me at work and asked me to come down here. What do you think he wants? You should know more than me," my dad interrogated.

I was about to answer him when the principal came strutting in. He quickly closed the door and sat down behind the desk.

"Mr. and Mrs. Johnson, thank you both for coming down here on such short notice. I know that we have discussed Nicholas' behavioral challenges before. I want to give you my word that we have made every effort to correct and guide Nicholas onto the path of productivity. I regret that due to obsessive truancy, tardies and belligerent behavior, we are asking you to find another avenue of education for Nick."

"What's he saying, Mom?" I asked, unable to decipher his meaning.

My mom kept her gaze on Mr. Jacobs, but answered me. "I believe what he is saying is that you are being expelled. Is that right?"

"Yes, ma'am, that is right. You may settle any outstanding fees at the front desk and clean out his locker before 3 p.m. today." With that, he stood and shook my parents' hands.

My mom choked out, "Thank you for all you've done for our son. We appreciate it."

I tried to convince myself that I didn't care, that I hated school. The truth was that being expelled was one more door slamming in my face in my search for a place to belong.

Each step I took on the shiny floors echoed as my parents' steps mimicked mine. I cleaned out my locker, and that was it.

A CRY TO BELONG

Principal Jacobs finally discovered what I had feared all along: I didn't belong in high school.

***

Even if I didn't fit in at high school, I at least felt at home with Matt and the guys. Smoking weed with my friends and hanging out felt like being part of a family, for a while. I would still come on campus every now and then. That's where I met Julie.

Julie was the coolest chick I knew. She smoked weed with us, and she didn't always want you to change like all the rich, straight-laced girls I knew.

I would do anything to be with my friends. My parents blamed them for my escalating drug abuse, but Matt and Julie were simply two other drugs I was using to ease the pain. I had already lost high school. I desperately fought against losing anything or anyone else.

"Nicholas, please don't go out with those kids. We know they are druggies, and you're better than that. Please, I'm begging you," my mom implored.

"Mom, you don't even know Matt. I'll be back by midnight," I explained.

"Nick, I'm not begging you. I'm telling you not to go. I don't like them. You're not the same. Don't walk out that door, Nick!" my father demanded.

"See you later," I assured, closing the door behind me.

We sat in a circle, smoking weed at Matt's house, when Julie touched my upper thigh. We were both so high that we just went with it. Having sex with a friend was almost comfort, somewhat close to peace. It wasn't what I needed, but it was a convincing imposter.

My body was still humming from the drugs, and the smell of smoke and sex clung to my clothes when I finally got to my house. My old boy scout backpack was full and sitting on the dimly lit porch. My dad, who had been waiting for me, came out on the porch.

"Hey, Nick, your mother and I think it's best that you move out. We know you're doing drugs with that Matt boy, and we just can't let that kind of stuff go on under our roof. We're thinking of the whole family. Your brothers can't be exposed to this kind of behavior, either," he explained stoically, though tears ran down his cheeks.

With that, my mom, who had been listening from inside, joined us on the porch. I stared at her, unable to comprehend what was going on. She turned her back on me. She was my mom.

I didn't realize at the time that my addiction had already let them down and destroyed their faith in my success. They, too, were feeling betrayed.

"Nicholas, we have filled your backpack with clothes, some food and a few bucks. We're going to drive you to the station. We're sure you'll do fine," my mom explained, through her muffled sobs.

"You gotta be kidding me. This is a bunch of crap. My own parents are kicking me out? What kind of parents are you? You're just going to quit on me?" I accused.

"We aren't quitting on you. You are the one who quit a long time ago, Nick. You're welcome back the minute you clean up your act," my dad replied.

"When I clean up my act? So, I have to fit into some mold before I can live with you? Maybe I should leave then," I said out of frustration with him and with my own addictions.

The backseat was dark and cold as we sat in silence. I wanted time to move slower, for the MAX light rail station sign to never come into view. I didn't want to leave my parents' house, but I didn't want to stay, either.

When the car tires slowed to a stop, the knot in my stomach tightened. My legs shook as I exited. I reached back in to grab my backpack with my sweaty hands and thrust it onto my weary back.

My parents' eyes were filled with tears. My heart was filled with anger. But all three of us were empty.

"We love you, Nicky," my mother assured me.

I watched their taillights until they disappeared, like in one of those cheesy movies from the 80s. I couldn't help but notice my mom starting to cry as they pulled away into the dark night.

***

"You know, Julie, we really have it pretty good here. I mean, I finally got a job at the pizza place, and I'm not couch hopping every night," I said while we were waiting for our friends to come over to our condo for a party.

"I guess. I mean, don't you think we fight too much? If you weren't such a jerk and an a**h*** all the time, maybe we'd have it even better," Julie said, smiling.

I laughed but wasn't completely convinced she was joking.

The months of wandering were starting to make that slow, treacherous journey from experience to memory. Perhaps Julie and I living together would erase the cold nights spent sleeping on park benches, struggling to find a joint, let alone a bag of weed.

The doorbell rang, and within minutes, our condo was filled with our friends all coming with beer or weed. Matt came with his water bong. Shelly, one of Julie's friends, brought a party ball. It was great.

Smoke hung thick in the air, and the walls vibrated in time with the music as I looked around for Julie. How long had it been since I had last seen her? I was too high to be able to gauge time, but it seemed like at least an hour since I saw her and Shelly go into a back room.

Maybe Shelly had brought more than a party ball, and they were getting high. What kind of girlfriend doesn't share her drugs?

I made my way down the narrow hall to see if there were any drugs left, or if Shelly and Julie had used them all. I opened the door, jokingly accusing them of smoking all the weed in the house.

"Hey, you two. You can't just sit back here all night and smoke ..." My voice trailed off, as I stood, shocked at what I saw.

Julie and Shelly were in our bed together. My entrance had startled them to sitting, but the disheveled hair and the twisted sheets declared the cruel truth.

I couldn't bear to look at them, so I stared at the clothes, hastily discarded in piles on the side of the bed.

"I think you need to get out, and take your little lesbian girlfriend with you!" I was enraged and felt betrayed.

Then, I turned and went back out into the living room, unable to face Julie anymore. Julie and Shelly walked out, not making eye contact with anyone.

"Dude, what happened? Why is Julie leaving?" Matt asked.

"Because she's a lying whore!" I yelled, turning to punch a hole in the wall of my living room.

But as my fist penetrated the sheetrock, I felt no better. Why had it not worked out?

Now, I was left with only holes and emptiness.

"Hey, what happened?" Matt slurred the question, almost too high to listen to the reply.

"She was in there messing around with Shelly!"

"Screw her, dude. Take another hit, and put all this crap behind you," Matt coaxed.

As I inhaled deep and the numbness encircled my mind, I had a nagging suspicion that I wouldn't be able to put it all behind me. Who could? I knew I couldn't stay high forever, and when I sobered up, Julie would still be gone. I would again be alone, surrounded by the mess I had made.

***

I did my very best to stay high, so high I could forget the pain of the betrayal and the loneliness that tormented me. But I also stayed high enough to lose my job and my home. Living in the woods and smoking pot, my bitter isolation cut far deeper than the chilled night air. I could build a fire for my bones, but there was no warmth for my frozen soul.

I watched my breath hover in half-frozen clouds as my frigid fingers weighed baggies of pot to sell that day. I'd sell enough to pay for a hot dog at the park and a pack of cigarettes. The rest would end up in the bowl of my pipe.

As I made my way to Pioneer Courthouse Square, where all the street kids hung out near the city park, a man was standing by the pillar where so many of the drug deals went down. He immediately caught my attention. He looked up from his feet long enough to make eye contact. I nodded, crossing the walkway to reach him.

"How much you want today?" I asked.

"Whatcha got?" my customer inquired.

"I got dimes and quarter bags." I proudly announced my inventory.

"I'll take a dime bag," he ordered.

I put the dime bag in his left hand, while his right hand came out of his pocket with a set of handcuffs. The cuff was around my wrist before the bag of pot had left my other hand.

A CRY TO BELONG

"You have the right to remain silent," he began as I stood there in utter disbelief.

***

The dark night enveloped me as I huddled by a tree to keep warm. The short time I spent in jail wasn't as hard as enduring the cold nights sleeping outside. As dusk gave way to darkness and one day yielded to the next, I decided to go home again.

I knocked at the door loudly, knowing my dad would be asleep at 2 a.m. Nervously, I shifted my weight back and forth on my swollen feet.

"Nick, you're alive? Come in out of the cold. You're going to freeze to death out there," my dad said.

The dim light of a solitary lamp glowed in the living room while we talked about the last year. He was glad I was safe, and I was glad I was warm.

"I want to move back in. I'll do whatever you want. I can't live outside anymore," I admitted.

"You can live here, but you have to go into rehab first," my dad ordered.

Rehab was unsuccessful, so it was only a matter of time before I was using drugs again. At least I had a roof over my head for a little while, as long as I made sure not to smell like pot when I came home.

***

"Nick, it's totally cool that you could help with rent and s***," my buddy Mark said as we moved my stuff into his extra bedroom.

"I just couldn't stay there anymore, you know? I mean, I should be able to live my life and all," I justified my move to Mark.

"Now that we've got the unpacking done, you want to smoke some weed? We could smoke as much as we want, and then save the rest for my buyers coming by later tonight."

"That sounds like a plan to me, dude," I said, content that this arrangement would be awesome.

The worn couch slouched to cocoon me as I spent the evening watching TV and getting high. Mark was out at the clubs trying to sell some Ecstasy before the next batch came in. Food commercials kept coming on, until the pot munchies drove me to the kitchen.

Standing in the cold path of the open freezer door, I saw what looked like frozen little candies. Score! I was so hungry that I ate almost half of the candy and lay down to sleep on my bed.

Searing pain registered in my brain long before I even opened my eyes. Razor sharp pangs scissored through my abdomen as I lay writhing on my bed. Something was really wrong.

My quivering fingers fumbled as I tried frantically to call my dad. I was scared and in pain, and I needed my dad. His voice sounded strange and distant, despite the clear connection.

"Dad, it's Nick. Something's really wrong. Dad, I think I'm dying. Come help me. Please take me to the hospital," I begged.

"Nicholas, is this drug related?" my dad inquired hesitantly.

"I don't know. I just ate something in the freezer, and now I hurt. Help me!" I cried.

"I'm on my way over," assured my dad.

Curled tightly in the fetal position, sweat streamed down my face. The room started to lose its reality, and I went back and forth between authentic and dream.

My father's heavy fist knocking on the door sounded as if it came from inside my own head, though the pounding of my own heartbeat seemed a million miles away. His worried face peering over me seemed distorted and scary.

"C'mon, let's get you some help," my dad ordered as he boosted me up and helped me make my way to the car.

The colorful street signs smeared into a blurred rainbow as my father and I sped to the hospital. Within minutes, the burn of tranquilizer shots stung a path up my arm and slowed the progression of the hallucinations.

"Can I call Mark?" I mumbled.

The phone felt heavy and cold against my cheek.

"Mark, what the h*** was in the freezer?" I asked.

"Dude, you didn't eat it did you?" Mark said in disbelief.

"Yes, man. About half. What of it?" I questioned my roommate.

"You dumb idiot! That was acid, man!" Mark scolded.

"You should have warned me, dude," I said as the doctor entered the room.

"Well, you're going to be okay. We've given you some tranquilizers. The pain in your stomach is pretty customary with ingesting that much LSD," explained the doctor. "We're going to release you. Take it easy, and please look into a rehabilitation program."

***

"How long you been working here?" the pretty girl at my new job asked me.

"This is my first week," I stammered without making eye contact.

"You like to party?" she asked, leaning closer.

"Sure."

"Party with me."

Tiffany and I partied that night. I felt kind of bad with her kids there. I may have been an addict, but I didn't want to mess up kids. But her children didn't even seem to notice the odd behavior of their stoned mother as she knocked the pipe off the coffee table, casting small red embers onto the carpet of the trailer. Her 4-year-old daughter stood up, unaffected, to get ready for bed and to hand the little boy a bottle.

Selina's little brown eyes stared blankly as I came out of her mother's bedroom the next morning wearing only my boxers. She didn't even question my presence when I sat at the table to eat a bowl of cereal.

How much did she know? Was I just one more man emerging from the bedroom, as commonplace as her cartoons, but simply not as interesting?

Staying late, getting high and having sex became a daily routine. Routine became a living arrangement. The kids didn't seem to mind me living there, although they didn't like it, either.

It wasn't long before we had a reputation for partying, and the drug dealers came around in droves.

Charlie, a meth dealer from the same trailer park, came to party and offered us some meth. Meth was cool. We could stay up all week and smoke more weed.

We moved to an apartment, but the meth train seemed to have tracks that led to our front door.

JOURNEY TOWARD FREEDOM

***

"Where you been? Upstairs buying meth from James again?" I asked my new wife, while giving Steven a piece of bread and taking another hit on our bong.

"What difference does it make? Now that we're married, do you think you can control me or something?" Tiffany asked, growing more agitated. Things became really strained emotionally as the months of her meth use stretched into years.

"I was just asking. I don't give a s*** where you were. I was just asking. Now give me the meth and shut up," I ordered.

I took the meth from her shaking hand, eyeing her pregnant belly peeking out of her tight t-shirt. She gave it to me and walked back out the door and up the stairs to James' apartment.

I didn't care where she was, as long as I was sky high. The kids would just watch my head nod as I would slowly slip into oblivion. Tiffany wouldn't be back for hours, and I wouldn't be sober for days.

***

"James, can't we work out an agreement on the price?" Tiffany asked as she leaned forward to reveal her chest, while she rubbed his thigh.

"Oh, little lady, I love the way you think. I'm sure we could work it out in trade," James agreed.

***

"Open up, this is the police!" a voice shouted through our apartment door.

Tiffany looked through the peephole and shot me a panicked look.

"It's the cops, and they have social workers with them. We're going down, Nick," she explained.

I stood up and ran frantically toward the bedroom. My shaking fingers struggled with the window as I heard the men enter the living room.

Pine needles embedded in my legs as I landed on a bush and began to run. My heavy, drug-laden steps didn't get me far.

A CRY TO BELONG

"Mr. Johnson, we advise you to get to the ground now," the booming voice ordered in the black night.

"We've had reports of drug activity at this address, and child welfare will now be handling the guardianship of the children," he later explained as we made the long, dark drive to the county jail.

***

"Hello?" I slurred, too drunk to answer the phone with much more of a greeting. My new roommate, Jack, a Vietnam vet, sat numbly watching TV.

"You need to come get your kids. Your ex never showed up to get them. We can't keep them forever. It was just supposed to be on weekends," my brother explained.

"Dude, Jeff, I can't take them, either. I mean, I just got divorced. I just can't, man," I answered.

"You're a jerk, Nick. You won't stay sober long enough to think about anyone else. You're not the brother I grew up with. You know, I don't even consider you family anymore. You're dead to me, Nick. Dead to me!" he screamed. The slamming of the phone echoed in my ear for minutes, in my soul for years.

I drank deep of the 40-ounce bottle I'd been holding. Jack just looked at me.

I stood up quickly, grabbed my jacket and headed for the door. "I'm going to go score some weed. I'll be back later."

***

No matter how much weed I scored or how much I drank, nothing could mend the raw wound that Tiffany's adultery had inflicted. After the divorce was final, I kept searching for something to numb the searing pain of regret I carried from all the wrong choices I made, but there wasn't anything. I again didn't belong. I didn't belong with my wife or my kids. But by now, I didn't even belong to myself.

Pumping gas, smoking pot and getting drunk quickly made up my entire existence. My protective wall of celibacy was built with bitter bricks and hateful mortar.

My hand gripped the gas pump tighter as I stared into the noonday sun. My friend Sean was pumping within earshot.

"What you always staring at, man? You're going to get hit by one of these cars someday," Sean joked. We were trying to kill time until we could clock out and go get stoned.

"I don't know. I'm just thinking about stuff." I tried to make excuses for my daydreaming. I always dreamed of being accepted and successful. Those dreams gave me hope for the future but also made my present seem all the bleaker.

Emily Watson pulled up to the pump behind me as Sean and I walked inside. We'd let Charlie handle this one.

"Hey, dude, I see the way you're always looking at Emily. You're always too nervous to pump her gas, but you watch her walk like she's the stinkin' Queen of England," Sean kidded.

"Emily? Nah, get off it, I mean she's pretty and all but — nah," I fumbled, embarrassed that my affections had been so obvious.

"You loser! Go get her number," Sean coaxed.

"I'm not like that," I argued.

"Well, then be like that," Sean rebutted.

I nervously walked up to Emily's car as another employee pumped her gas. I leaned over her driver's window and asked for her number.

"I don't do that. Give me yours," Emily suggested.

"You'll never call me," I said.

"Probably not," she retorted with a bubbly grin that made my stomach tighten.

Two weeks later, her voice at the other end of the phone was the sweetest starting bell any great run has ever had. We talked for hours, days, months.

Emily was kind and happy. She was an excellent mother to her children and became a loyal friend and lover.

My rampant alcoholism and drug abuse masqueraded behind domestic life. I wore our weekly trips to the beach and bedtime stories as badges, proving that I didn't have a substance abuse problem. Our laughter and joy served as proof that I could handle my drinking and drugs. I watched her belly grow full with the life we created. The mask, however, was growing thin, and my bitterness could only be numbed for a season.

This charade was finally shattered when Emily asked me to quit smoking pot because our money had run out. I drank instead of smoking weed, but I drank more and more to make up for the lack of marijuana.

A CRY TO BELONG

***

I sat on the couch, waiting for her to get home from the grocery store with the beer to replace the empty one in my hand. I watched her pull up in the driveway with the three boys.

"Hey, babe. I can help you with the groceries," I offered to get to the beer quicker.

As she got close enough to smell my breath, her face showed obvious disappointment. "Are you drunk already?" She asked the question that she already knew the answer to.

"Hey, it's Saturday. I can drink if I want to," I responded.

"Boys, go to your rooms and play while Daddy and I have a talk," Emily ordered. The boys' quick feet made their way out of the conflict.

"You need to stay out of my stinking business. I'm tired, and I want a beer. Look, I'm not an axe murderer, Emily!" I stammered, trying to defend my behavior.

"Nick, I'm really worried about you. You're drinking a lot," she responded softly.

"Give me the beer," I said, reaching out my hand.

"I won't." She defiantly refused to let go of my beer.

We squared off in the living room. She blocked the front door so I couldn't get to the groceries in the car.

"Get out of my way," I commanded.

"I won't," she repeated.

"Would you lighten up and get off my back, Emily?" I screamed as I punched the window. The shards of glass embedded in my fist were numbed by the alcohol and rage.

"I think you need to leave. The kids are terrified. You are an alcoholic, and I need you to leave. Don't call until you get some help," she asserted.

I left, grabbing the beer out of the car on my way out. I left alone and drunk, the way I had always been, the way I feared I would always be.

***

I shut the door to my small apartment to go score some weed when I decided to go to Edith Sterling's house instead.

Her kind, loving face greeted me with love as it always had since I was married to Tiffany.

"Nicholas, how are you? Are you still with Emily and the boys?" she asked, sincerely concerned about me.

"No, that didn't work out," I said, hanging my head.

"Well, come on in, and let's talk about it," she invited.

The warm coffee and conversation Edith provided had become a touchstone for me ever since she had moved next door to Tiffany and me. The lines on her face were from smiling, not worrying. That confused me but gave me hope.

"You know, Nick, my church has a Celebrate Recovery group. I think we both know your issues with Tiffany and Emily were drug and alcohol related. I was only a neighbor, but even I could see that."

"Miss Sterling, I appreciate your kindness, your hugs and all the times you've told me about God. But I'm not interested in your little church group, okay?" I said nicely, but firmly.

"Good enough. Want another cup of coffee, dear?" she said as kind as always.

***

I stood looking at the door of the church, hesitant to go in, but not willing to endure four more weeks of Edith's persistent invitations.

A young woman greeted me at the door of Celebrate Recovery and asked me my story. I said that I had been off meth for four years and had come to give the members hope.

I could tell that she didn't believe me, but I was unable to be truthful about my addiction.

I sat down on the chairs in the midst of a crowd that looked like me. It was closer to belonging than I had ever dared to come before. Tears ran down my cheeks as I listened to the stories of freedom and love. This Jesus, this God had saved them all. Was God calling me to belong to this group of "freed" ones?

The smell of smoke and stale beer accosted my senses when I opened my apartment door. Their testimonies replayed in my head as I sat on my couch looking at a picture on the nearby wall. The illustrious dragon was escaping from the fiery destruction he had ignited. I stared deeper.

A CRY TO BELONG

A voice, strong and angry, echoed in my mind. *You are already destroyed. There is no freedom for mere ashes.*

"Shut up!" I cried, and I punched the glass, spraying blood along the wall.

Another voice spoke softly to my heart. *Go to the hospital. It'll be just fine.*

I left my apartment bloody and broken. As I walked to the emergency room, I punched every wall in my path, exposing bone and muscle in my wounded fist.

The doctor paid no heed to my story of the voices as he pulled the thread through my knuckles. He was more interested in mending my skin. But I needed a doctor to heal my soul.

On the long walk back to my lonely apartment, I walked through drug-infested neighborhoods and past prostitute-laden corners. And I thought about all the testimonies I had heard at Celebrate Recovery. I could see clearly the box of marijuana and the empty liquor bottles for what they really were. They were the steel bars of my prison, and I wanted out.

The splattered blood soaked into my jeans from the carpet as I fell to my knees. "God," I sobbed, "you gotta help me. I'll do anything — anything. You gotta get me out of here."

Warmth spread through my entire body as God began the process of healing my soul. I fell asleep peacefully for the first time in years.

As the morning sun shone through the curtains to wake me, I was surprised by the joy I felt in my heart. I knew everything would be all right, just like the kind voice had said.

***

My joy was so full and complete that I told everyone about Jesus. Drug dealers and alcoholics looked at me with the same hopeless confusion that I once had.

I volunteered at the church where I went to Celebrate Recovery, and they loved me and helped me grow in knowing God. Pastor John even invited me to live with him, since I worked at the church.

One day, while we were working, Pastor John mentioned Freedom House.

"It's a place of growth, Nick. You deserve complete wholeness, and I think you can grow deeper in Christ there," he explained with compassion.

I wanted to listen to him. I respected him, and I was living under his roof. But, this time, he was way off base.

"That's okay, Pastor John. Your kindness is helping me grow just fine. And besides, I'm already off drugs and alcohol." I politely declined the offer.

The same feeling of warmth that let me know God was listening that dark night in my apartment started to fill my body again. I knew what that meant. God agreed with Pastor John, and I wanted to agree with God.

As we drove together to Freedom House, Pastor John and I reminisced about all that Jesus had done for me.

"He's not done with you, Nick. You're still young. He's got more blessings in store for you," he assured me as we pulled into the parking lot of Freedom House.

***

I was sure that I was hearing and following God. The year at Freedom House was rich soil in which Jesus planted and cultivated the seeds of my healing.

The sweet lessons that I learned about God I will take with me always. All my life, I thought I wanted to belong with someone. I learned, among other things, that I don't belong *with*, I belong *to*. Humbly, I accepted the fact that I was not my own. I belonged *to* God, and it was great to belong.

***

"Without further *adieu*, I am proud to reward Nick Johnson for his full completion of 12 months in Freedom House," Jim said in his booming voice.

Astonished, I could barely make my feet carry me to the front to accept my graduation certificate and gifts. I turned to the crowd to see my brother stand and approach the podium to say something. My heart sank as I anticipated harsh words for all we had endured. Why had he even come if he hated me so? Wasn't I kind of like dead to him?

He cleared his throat while all in the room waited in expectation for what he was about to share. I held my breath and braced myself for the torrent of anger I deserved.

"When I came here tonight, I couldn't help but notice all the people and friends who came here for my brother Nick. I never knew that he had friends like this or that he had influenced so many people. When I first saw him tonight, I knew he was different. I like my new brother, and I look forward to getting to know him better."

I was shocked! My brother was actually hugging me. This was the very first time we had shown any familial affection or love in more than five years. I was expecting the worst, and God gave me the best by reuniting my brother and I. Healing was in the house. Freedom House. I could faintly hear the warm, soft voice of the Lord saying, *I told you it would be all right.*

And now, I know he's right.

FOUND AT LAST
The Story of Pat White
Written by Karen Koczwara

"Pat, can you hear me? Pat! Dude, I think he's dead."

Fuzzy voices outside the car window crackled around me like a radio with bad reception. I tried to open my eyes, but my head throbbed so badly I could hardly see. Where was I, and what on earth had happened?

"Is he breathing?"

"Help me get this door open, man. We gotta get him outta here quick."

"You mean what's *left* of the door. I've never seen anything like this, man. This thing is crushed like a pancake. Insane."

Crushed like a pancake? And I was still alive? Or was I? Was this all a dream, a nightmare perhaps? With what little strength I could muster, I attempted to move my left leg. A searing pain shot through my muscles, bringing tears to my eyes. *Oh, God, what's happening? Am I going to die?*

"He's moving, man. I think he's alive."

"I'm alive! I'm alive!" I tried to move my mouth to speak, but no words came out. My entire body felt like a giant brick, weighed down by an excruciating pain that didn't let up. Random images swirled through my mind. The beers I'd had, one after another. I'd lost track after number five. But where had I been? And how had I gotten here?

"Pat, hang in there, man. We're going to get you out!"

I squinted my eyes open and tried to make sense of the face in front of me. The blurred image looked slightly familiar, but I couldn't quite place it. "Help," I croaked, but again, no words escaped my lips. My entire body felt like it was on fire, a giant burning ember. Panicked, I turned my neck slowly to glance around the car. Maybe I really *was* on fire! *Oh, God, what's happening?! Help me!*

"He's definitely moving, man. I think I can get at him now."

Help me! Oh, please help! My limbs went weak, and I prayed I wouldn't lose consciousness. I didn't want to die. Not yet! Not this way! *God, help me!*

JOURNEY TOWARD FREEDOM

***

"Hey, man, I got somethin' for you to try." My brother pulled a cigarette from his pocket and handed it to me. "You're a big kid now. Think you can handle it?" He grinned and lit the end before I could protest.

I took the cigarette and held it gingerly between my two fingers as I'd seen people on television do. Not wanting to look awkward or apprehensive in front of my brother and his big junior high friend, I put the cigarette to my lips and inhaled.

"Nice. You look like a pro," my brother commended me, laughing.

The smoke burned as it went down, but I suppressed the urge to cough. "Not bad," I lied and took another drag. "Where did you get these, anyway?"

My brother glanced at his friend and shrugged. "Doesn't matter. There's more where they came from, though."

"Huh." I extended my arm, exhaled and hoped I looked cool. It wasn't every day my older brother let me hang out with his buddies, much less introduced me to things that were off limits. I didn't care for the cigarette but wasn't about to tell him that. Maybe the next one would go down easier. Or the next one. I had a feeling this wouldn't be my last smoke.

Born in Tillamook, Oregon, I was just a few months old when my parents divorced. My mother had three boys from a previous husband; I was the product of her second husband. She eventually remarried a man who had two daughters. Sandwiched into the middle of a Brady Bunch-like family, I struggled to find my place as a child.

When I turned 7 years old, my older brother turned me on to smoking cigarettes. They seemed harmless enough. Having been a quiet outsider most of my short life, I felt a strange urge to rebel against my family. Smoking seemed to fulfill this need.

One afternoon, my brothers coaxed me into the woods behind our house. "Come on, Pat. We want to show you something fun," they insisted, a mischievous twinkle in their eyes.

Curious, I trudged behind my brothers out past the yard and into the thick wooded area behind our house.

To my surprise, my younger sisters were waiting there, as well, playing in the dirt.

FOUND AT LAST

"All right. Here's how the game works. You take down your pants, for starters," one of my brothers said, grinning.

My heart skipped a beat. What was this all about? I glanced over at my sisters who looked up from their little game and frowned disapprovingly. "Ohh … kay," I muttered and did as they instructed. Where did the game part come in? And what did taking down my pants have to do with it?

"Good, good. Now get on top of your sister." My brother pointed down at my sister and nodded. "That's right. You heard me."

Now this was getting weird. I reached for my pants, but my brother shook his head, frowning. "Do it, Pat. Come on. Play along here."

Slowly, I dropped to the dirt and climbed on top of my sister, despite her horrified look. Something about this felt very, very wrong. Why, oh, why did I agree to come out here? I should have known my brothers were up to trouble. They only liked to get me involved when they needed an accomplice or wanted me to make a fool of myself.

"Now what?" I croaked. "Can I get up now?" Why was I asking their permission? My gut told me to jump to my feet and run. This was just not right.

My brother shrugged, suddenly disinterested in this little game. "I guess." He exchanged glances with my other brothers and they giggled.

Feeling suddenly sick, I hopped off my sister and yanked my pants to my waist, fastening my belt with shaking fingers. "That was stupid," I muttered. "Really stupid."

"Whatever." More giggles.

My sister glanced up at me with wide, terrified eyes. *Nothing happened,* I reasoned. It was just some stupid game with no point. No one got hurt. But as I drug my feet back home that afternoon, I felt sick in the pit of my stomach.

When I reached the fifth grade, I began experimenting with marijuana. My brother and his junior high friends made it easily accessible. Unlike my first cigarette, I enjoyed my first joint. The smoke went down easily without stinging my lungs, and within moments, I broke into a fit of laughter. Getting high, it turned out, was more fun than I'd imagined. My entire body relaxed, and I eased onto the sofa, smiling. I could definitely get used to this.

One day, I followed my brother over to his friend's house to smoke a joint. His buddy pulled out a stash of magazines from underneath his bed. "Now this stuff is the real deal," he chuckled, flashing one in my face. A near naked woman graced the cover. "Beautiful, eh? And this is only the cover. Wait till you see what's inside!"

"Where'd you get this stuff, man?" My brother snatched a magazine from his buddy's hand and flipped it open. He whistled under his breath as he turned the pages. "Man, almighty, so this is what we've been missin' out on all these years."

"Gimme one," I insisted, not wanting to be left out. I took a magazine and opened it slowly, as though a snake might jump out and bite me. Naked, beautiful women, page after page. It was every adolescent boy's fantasy. I tried to look away but found I couldn't. The pictures were fascinating.

"Whew! Check out the hottie on page 71!" My brother held up his magazine, and we all agreed with a whistle. "This is better than gold, man. How'd you get such a stash?"

His buddy raised an eyebrow. "I have my ways."

I liked being part of this inner circle, the little brother getting a peek at his big brother's sophisticated world. Cigarettes, pot and now porn magazines! The important thing was to keep looking cool so as not to lose my inner circle status.

"This stuff is nice," I agreed. "Very nice."

Junior high rolled around, and I graduated from pot to inhalants. My father was a painter, and obtaining his paint thinner was easier than expected. I enjoyed the quick high I got off of sniffing glue, as well.

It was surprising how easy it was to get high off of typical household products. Before long, I found myself rummaging around cupboards and drawers in search of the next thing I could sniff.

School became less interesting to me the more I smoked and inhaled. I began ditching on a regular basis, often retreating to friends' houses to have a joint or share a can of paint thinner with them. I enjoyed the secret little life I led and wondered how long I'd be able to go on fooling my parents.

One afternoon, I came home to find my mother sitting on the couch, glaring at me. "Where were you today, Pat?" she demanded, hands on hips.

FOUND AT LAST

I shrugged and tried to appear nonchalant. "What are you talking about?" I asked coolly.

"Don't try to lie to me, son," she replied. "The school called. I know you were gone today. And a few other days, apparently. Just what makes you think you can skip school? This is completely unacceptable."

I stared at the floor, fumbling for an answer. "Um, sorry?" There was no use denying it. I'd been caught. I waited for my mother to bring up the smoking, but she didn't. Before this conversation could continue, I escaped to my bedroom and shut the door. A sigh of relief escaped my lips. I had to keep up a better front, at least for a few weeks. No use in upsetting my parents. They already suspected my brothers were trouble.

One evening, my brothers and sisters and I had a sleepover in the living room. When our parents were safely in bed and the lights were out, my brother leaned over to me and whispered, "Go get in the sleeping bag with your sister."

"No," I whispered back defiantly. I wasn't about to succumb to his little "games" again.

"Do it. Now." Even in the dark, I could see his "I mean it or else" look.

Slowly, I rose from my sleeping bag and slid into my sister's, who slept peacefully beside me.

"Now tickle her," he whispered. "Lift up her shirt and tickle her."

Now this felt plain wrong. I jumped out of the sleeping bag and returned to my own. "Enough," I sneered and turned over to go to sleep. "Leave me alone."

"Wimp." My brother snorted and turned over.

Tears stung my eyes as I tossed and turned. I hated my brother pushing me into things I didn't want to do. Smoking was one thing, but taking advantage of my sisters was another. I couldn't let this go on!

A few days later, I approached my mother hesitantly. "I need to talk to you about something," I said slowly.

My mother looked up from her newspaper and nodded. "Yes, Pat?"

"I, uh, I, well, the truth is, the older boys are trying to force me to, uh, do stuff with the girls, and I don't like it."

I waited for the look of horror on my mother's face, but she simply put her paper down and frowned. "Well, just don't do it. Just ignore them. They don't have a gun to your head, do they?"

I shook my head, disappointed in her less-than-emotional reaction. That was it? That was all I was going to get?

"All right, well, I just thought you should know." I slunk from the kitchen table and decided to keep things to myself from now on.

***

My family moved from Oregon to Colorado, and then to Indiana for a year. I stopped doing drugs in Indiana, as I didn't have any friends to do them with.

We relocated back to Colorado during the latter part of my junior high years, and I resumed my usual ways.

"You goin' to the city fair in Grand Junction tonight?" One of my buddies called me one Friday evening. "Don't tell me you have somethin' better to do."

"Nah. I'll meet you there." I grabbed a pack of cigarettes and headed out the door. Friday nights were usually uneventful, but perhaps tonight we'd meet a few girls at the fair and have a good time.

The rides were in full swing when I arrived. Country music blared in the background, and bright lights dotted the usually sleepy fields now transformed into a giant fair. I found my buddy, and we hopped on the Ferris wheel. I pulled out my smokes and lit a cigarette. The cool breeze whipped at my cheeks as we went round and round.

"I got somethin' better than that," my buddy whispered, patting his pocket. He pulled out an innocent looking sugar cube. "Ever tried one of these babies?"

I stared at him. "Sugar cube? What's the big deal?"

"Not just any sugar cube," he chuckled. "Acid, man. Will take you on the best trip of your life, if you know what I mean."

I finished my cigarette and popped the cube in my mouth. It seemed harmless enough. Within minutes, however, I was spinning right along with the Ferris wheel. The ground beneath me was a blur of brightly colored dots and lines as I peered over the edge.

FOUND AT LAST

Okay, what is this crazy s***?" I murmured, staring at my buddy. His face looked like a clown's. This was unlike any joint I'd ever smoked!

My buddy just laughed. "Told you you'd like it."

This was just the beginning for me. Speed followed, then mushrooms, better known as "shrooms." When I couldn't get my hands on these drugs, I opted for inhalants. Carburetor cleaner was always an easy one to snag. A few whiffs and I was flying high for the night. I enjoyed the high I got off each drug, the way I felt light and happy. The introverted, insecure boy of my childhood seemed a distant stranger when I was sniffing or drinking.

When I turned 16, I moved out, got my driver's license and bought a brand new car. I felt like a million bucks driving around in a car all my own. I lived with different friends and found a job working nights as a grocery store janitor.

It was easy money, and the late night shifts gave me the opportunity to keep up with my drug habit. There was also a tempting supply of beer stocked in the store. I began swiping a few cans here and there, figuring no one would notice. The beer, I found, went down nicely with a joint or inhalant.

One night, after nearly everyone had left the store, I snuck out to my car, grabbed a can of carburetor cleaner and locked myself in the bathroom out back. I inhaled a few times, waiting for the high to kick in. Staying high made the night pass much more quickly.

The next thing I knew, someone was pounding on the bathroom door. My eyes flew open, and I stumbled to my feet. I had passed out cold on the hard bathroom floor! Half-conscious, I yanked open the bathroom door and found the produce manager staring back at me.

"You all right, man?" he asked, furrowing his brow. "You been gone a long time." His eyes wandered to the ground, where the can of carburetor cleaner sat beside my feet.

Trying to appear coherent, I launched into an explanation. "I just, uh, I must have fallen asleep for a minute," I replied quickly. "I, uh, I'll be right back in."

My fellow employee stared at me skeptically. "Yeah. Uh huh." He shrugged and stalked off.

My heart caught in my throat. I couldn't afford to lose this job! I had a car payment and a drug habit to keep up! Unfortunately, word got back to the store manager, and my job at the grocery store ended.

One afternoon, a few buddies of mine decided to ditch school and head out to a local shooting gallery. Not a big fan of school myself, I decided to join along, even offering to drive.

"Let's see. Advanced Algebra or Beer n Shooting Hour?" my buddy joked as we careened around a corner. He pulled a six-pack of beer from the backseat and popped one open.

"That's a no-brainer," I laughed. I grabbed a beer and took a long swig. It felt good to hit the open road. Who needed school, anyway, when there was more fun to be had drinking?

A few hours later, we sped back home. I'd had more than my share of beers but reasoned I could hold my liquor better than most guys. Suddenly, an unexpected curve jumped out of nowhere, and I found myself scrambling to gain control of the wheel. Moments later, the car careened into a ditch and tipped onto its side.

Heart thudding, I gripped the wheel with both hands and kept my foot steady on the brake. "You guys all right?" I croaked. I glanced out at the gravel in which we'd come to a screeching halt. "Thank God." It could have been a person, a building, or worse yet, another car.

My head throbbed, but I seemed to be otherwise unharmed. I climbed out of the car to observe the damage. It appeared we weren't going anywhere. The car was stuck nice and good in the ditch. I sank to my feet and shook my head. How had I gotten us into this mess? If only I'd been paying more attention!

"I'll go and call the wrecker," my buddy suggested. "You stay here with the car."

A strong wind stirred up out of nowhere, whipping at my shoulders as I sat waiting. Still reeling from the liquor and the accident, I tried to think clearly for a moment. Surely the cops wouldn't show up! And if they did, I'd just play it cool like I'd done so many times before.

There was no getting off easy this time, though. The cop who met me at the scene was less than amused with my little scenario.

"You been drinking, son?" the cop asked, glaring at me.

"Uh, I had a beer a few hours ago," I fibbed. Beads of perspiration popped out on my forehead.

"And the three rifles in the backseat there? You care to explain those?"

FOUND AT LAST

"We were, uh, shooting at the local gallery," I explained. *Play it cool, and everything will be all right.*

"I'm going to need you to step over here and walk the line," the cop replied, obviously not satisfied with my response.

Hours later, I found myself in a jail cell staring at a dirty, hard cement floor. My hands shook as I wrought them in my lap, praying the cops would have mercy on me and not slap me with a DUI. I couldn't afford to lose my license.

The cops gave me a well deserved DUI and revoked my license. Upset at the turn of circumstances, I moved back to Oregon to live with my brother, who had accepted Jesus into his heart and was now living with a different moral code than before. He talked often about his faith in God.

"This is a fresh start for you, Pat," he encouraged me. "You don't have to live in your old ways anymore. God can restore your life for you if you'll let him."

I mulled over my brother's words. I desperately wanted to give up my drinking and drugs and get my life straight. Perhaps I should give God a chance. I began attending church with my brother and even helped my sister in the Sunday school class. I noticed everyone at church seemed to be happy and fulfilled. Was I really missing out on something?

One night, after I'd downed a few beers, I curled up in a ball on my bed and stared at the wall. Tears rolled down my cheeks as I sobbed. "What am I doing?" I moaned, my insides aching along with my heart.

Suddenly, the room seemed to light up, and a warmth ran through my veins. It was as if I had come straight into the presence of the Lord.

"Lord, if you're here, please help me. I give my life to you, just like the preacher said. Please come into my life and help me." The moment I uttered the words, I felt a strange peace wash over me.

"Thank you, Lord," I whispered, falling back on the bed. "You are real!"

I continued going to church and helping with the Sunday school class. I didn't learn how to delve into my Bible, however, and didn't grow in my relationship with God. It wasn't long before I found myself sneaking off to smoke pot and drink again.

A horrible wreck nearly took me into eternity — the one where my door was crushed like a pancake and I barely made it out alive. I took a risk that night just by driving, as my license had already been revoked for drinking and driving. I guess it was the favor of God that I lived and simply landed in jail with a DUI for 30 days after a few days in the hospital.

You would think I had learned something from this, but soon, I was back on the road, driving to nowhere fast.

Inside my mind, a battle waged. I knew that God was the answer to my problems. I had seen the difference he'd made in my brothers' lives. But my addictive personality remained the thorn in my side. Getting high felt good. And I wasn't sure I could stop.

Afraid I might be in over my head, I checked into a 30-day recovery program. During this time, a pretty girl caught my attention, and it wasn't long before we began dating. Deep down, I knew I was in no place to be involved in a relationship, but I was lonely, and she filled that void.

My girlfriend, Roxanne, drank, and it didn't take long for me to join in with her. Our nights were spent in front of the television, downing liquor and making halfway sober conversation. A few months into our relationship, we learned she was pregnant. I wasn't terribly surprised.

"Now what?" I muttered one night as she sat cross-legged near me, her belly protruding. She already had two children from a previous relationship.

"Now we have a baby," she replied, laughing.

I wasn't so sure we were ready for this but figured it was too late to turn things around now. Roxanne gave birth to a beautiful little girl a few months later. I was elated to be a father, but the tension worsened between us. Money grew tight, and it seemed we couldn't agree on anything.

One evening, I had come to my wit's end with our relationship. I downed a few beers and headed outside in front of our townhouse. Life was no longer worth living. I attached a hose to the back of my car and closed the doors, waiting for the fumes to lull me to sleep for good.

"What are you doing, Pat? Are you crazy?!" Roxanne came storming outside toward me. "You're crazy, I tell you!" she screamed. She called the police, who showed up shortly after and took me to the psychiatric ward at the hospital.

"I'm not crazy," I insisted during my evaluation. *Just lonely.* I didn't voice the words, but they echoed in my head as I headed home a few days later. Even a girlfriend and a new baby could not fill the gaping hole in my life.

It didn't take long before Roxanne and I went our separate ways. She continued to party hard and lost custody of all of the children following our breakup. I was saddened at the loss, but even this didn't stop me from drinking.

A few weeks later, loneliness consumed me once again. I downed a few beers and found a gun under my bed. With trembling hands, I put it to my mouth. Death was just a click away.

Tears filled my eyes as my fingers hovered over the trigger. Life didn't seem worth living, but did I have the guts to end it? I took a deep breath and finally put the gun down. The glossy black object glared up at me, a terrifying reminder that I'd come inches from death. I could not continue on this roller coaster.

I entered another treatment program voluntarily a few months later, hoping to clean up my act once and for all. Inside the program, I had ample time to think about my life and my decisions. I was unhappy, searching for that missing piece of the puzzle to fulfill me. So far, drinking and drugs hadn't proved to be it, but would I ever be able to appease my loneliness inside?

While I struggled to find my place in the world, the rest of my siblings thrived in their lives. My brothers were now living for the Lord, happily married with children and good jobs. I often resented family get-togethers, for it pained me to see everyone happy when I was so miserable inside.

I was not yet ready to surrender to the very thing that gave them joy: a living relationship with Jesus Christ.

Wanting to rebel against my family and their values, I became involved in witchcraft. I found it especially fascinating. Before long, I had learned how — on full moons — to cast spells and use my cultic powers for selfish purposes. I became a white witch, or solitaire witch, and delved into the powerful, evil world of the occult. My dark world became even more disturbing when mixed with a few mushrooms or a hit of acid.

One evening, after blasting some evil music, my downstairs neighbor came up and asked me to turn the music down a bit. Anger rose in me, and I decided to hex him. I lit several candles and prepared to cast a spell on him. Moments later, another neighbor called and asked me to join him downstairs for a beer. I left the candles burning and went downstairs to join him.

JOURNEY TOWARD FREEDOM

When I returned upstairs, I found my apartment engulfed in flames, smoke billowing through the air as I threw open the door. Horrified, I pushed through the smoke, attempting to douse the fire before my entire apartment burned down. For the first time since I'd set foot into the world of witchcraft, I felt as though I'd pushed it too far with the other side. A darkness unlike anything I'd ever known overwhelmed me. Perhaps it was time to escape.

With my life going nowhere, I decided to head out into the woods and live as a hermit. I had worked at a clay factory and had obtained unemployment that would carry me over for a few months. With no rush to return to the working world, retreating to the wilderness for a while seemed like a good way to heal, think and process things.

I hiked out several miles into the woods until I came to the middle of nowhere. There, I set up a small tent that would serve as home for as long as I felt I needed. Climbing inside, I lay down and took a deep breath. The pine trees sang a soothing song as they rustled in the wind outside. A blue jay squawked in the distance, calling out for food. In the stillness of it all, I wondered if I might be able to get used to this sort of lifestyle.

For the next few weeks, I hiked around the area, taking pictures and exploring the untouched Oregon woods. With each step I took, I thought about my life. How had I gotten here, living as a hermit miles away from civilization? Would I ever find what I was truly looking for? Or did I even *know* what I was looking for?

I'd spent the last few years jumping from one drug to another, getting high, living life in the fast lane. My life had become a whirlwind of senseless activity. I needed a purpose, a reason to wake up each morning.

"It's all society's fault," I mumbled one night as I pulled off my boots and climbed inside my tent. An owl hooted somewhere off in the woods, and I felt lonelier than ever. "This stupid world is a joke."

I thought of my brother and wondered if he might be missing me back home. His words once again rang in my head as I tramped through the muddy trails. "God can restore your life, Pat …"

The Lord had done that for him; I wondered if it was really possible to restore my life or had God perhaps given up on me long ago?

FOUND AT LAST

When I finally tired of the long, scruffy beard I'd grown out and the deafening silence of the woods, I returned to the city. It was time to face the real world again. I had no idea what lay ahead for me, but one thing was for certain: I needed to move forward.

I found work at the Battle Creek Golf Course as an assistant groundskeeper. My job entailed watering and maintaining the large grounds at the facility. The biggest perk to the job was the free house I was able to live in directly on the golf course. It was a dream come true for a guy who needed a fresh start.

With no rent expenses, I found I had plenty of money to spend on other luxuries. These luxuries included meth and cocaine. I was surprised at how easy it was to get my hands on these drugs. Before long, I was back to my old ways. Only this time, things were more serious.

Meth was a new friend to me; I enjoyed the burst of energy it provided. Suddenly, I was able to do my job in record time. I maintained a decent front on the outside, while inside, I began to waste away once again.

A fellow employee made cocaine and meth easily accessible to me. He insisted I pay with cash at first, but when money got tight, I began pawning off my precious possessions in exchange for a little white bag of powder. My beloved Pioneer stereo, pellet gun and Game Cube were lost in a swift transaction.

Heroin was the next friend I met. I had sworn I'd never use needles, but before long, I found myself shooting up whenever I could. On more than one occasion, desperate to get high, I used bent needles. I even shared a needle with a guy who had Hepatitis C and contracted the disease. Deep down, I knew I was playing a dangerous game, but the high I got off my drugs won over any reservations I had.

One morning, I woke up with a terrible fever. My entire body ached, and I felt as though an elephant had settled himself on my chest. Each time I coughed, my insides felt like they were on fire. Tears welling in my eyes, I mustered all the strength I could to climb out of bed and call the doctor.

As it turned out, I had a severe case of pneumonia. My normally average frame wasted away to a mere 110 pounds in the next few weeks.

My eyes were like hollow sockets, and my ribs protruded through my t-shirts. For the first time, it occurred to me that I could die. I had abused my body for so many years, it was a wonder I hadn't ended up worse off.

Having hit this new low, I recognized it was time to do something about my drug habit once and for all.

"I need help," I told one of my managers desperately. "I can't go on like this."

"I know this great place in Eugene," he encouraged me. "You should give it a try."

"If this doesn't work, I'll totally understand if you have to let me go," I replied softly. I loved my job at the Battle Creek Golf Course and had managed to become a reliable employee, despite my abusive lifestyle outside work. The idea of having to leave and start over again was unbearable, but I knew I had to grasp hold of this opportunity.

The rehab center in Eugene proved helpful. The employees were kind to me and helped me work through some of my addictive behavior issues. When the time came for me to leave, I knew I still needed more help but wasn't sure where to turn next.

"There's this other place called Freedom House I've heard great things about," my brother Scott told me. "It's a Christian facility and focuses on helping you restore or find a relationship with God."

God. I hadn't thought much about God lately. I'd been too busy living my life as I pleased. Besides, he'd probably given up on me long ago. How could he still want to hang around to wait for a guy like me to get his act together?

"Nah, there's this other place I want to check out first," I told my brother. "But thanks, though. I'll keep it in mind."

I entered another rehab facility and spent the next couple of months there. It wasn't long, however, before I began fooling around with drugs again. I entered into another love-hate relationship with meth. It made me terribly withdrawn, but I loved it because it gave me a newfound energy that no amount of coffee could ever offer. I tried telling myself I could keep up a double life, doing drugs at night and working hard by day, but the truth was I was slowly losing my battle. Something would have to give. I could not simply go on fooling everyone, including myself, into thinking I had my act together.

One night, after taking a big hit, I heard a voice out of nowhere. Thinking one of my buddies had come to join me, I opened the front door, but my porch was empty. Then I heard the voice again, and then another, then another. Looking around me frantically, I tried to figure out where they were coming from. The whispers turned into wails, and I flung myself onto the couch, terrified. *What is going on?*

Suddenly, large footprints appeared on the ceiling, rows and rows of black footprints stretching from one wall to another. I gasped and dug my fingernails into my palms. This was beyond strange now; it was plain terrifying! I was in way over my head.

"Stop it! Stop it!" I cried out, batting at the images that danced in front of me.

Meanwhile, the voices continued, a rising wail that pierced my eardrums. Was I going crazy? Was it ever going to stop?

I threw on my shoes and ran out onto the porch to get a breath of fresh air. To my relief, the golf course sat quietly before me, a stretch of manicured landscape, just the way I'd left it. Whew. Maybe I wasn't really going crazy.

I glanced back toward the house, where just moments ago I'd seen and heard horrible things. This was no fun house at the state fair. I decided right then and there I'd pushed things too far this time. I wouldn't be held captive by a drug that made me crazy!

The next morning, I awoke to a quiet house. I put my finger to my wrist to make sure I could still feel my pulse. It was still racing from last night's events. Breathing a sigh of relief, I lay back on the bed and closed my eyes.

"Lord, I know I haven't always been there, but I'm tired of living like this. I can't do this anymore. I need your help."

As the words tumbled out of my mouth, I wondered for a moment if God even heard my prayer. Would he still want anything to do with me after all these years we'd barely spoken? But moments later, an overwhelming sense of peace washed over me. The warmth I'd felt years ago when I called out to God returned. I knew right then and there what I had to do. I had to get to Freedom House.

***

The minute I walked in the doors of Freedom House, I knew this place was different. I could feel it: a warmth I hadn't felt at any other rehab center. From the cheery painted walls to the smiling employees, Freedom House boasted a sense of peace and security. Though I couldn't quite put my finger on it, I was sure this time was not going to be the same.

Over the next few weeks, I dove into the program unlike anything I'd ever experienced. With ample time to study the Bible and pray each morning, my relationship with God became stronger than ever. It was during these quiet moments that I asked the Lord to restore my life and bring me back into a living relationship with him.

"I don't ever want to go back, Lord," I prayed one morning as I flipped my Bible open. "I want to live for you each day. I want to be addicted to *you*, Lord, and only you. I want to crave your word to the point that I can't get enough of it. Please show me what you want me to do with my life going forward. I know my experiences are not in vain. You are faithful and will walk beside me in my new journey."

My eyes fell onto one of my favorite Bible verses, Philippians 4:13: "I can do all things through Christ who strengthens me." I read the words over and over, tears filling my eyes. *All* things! It was Christ who would strengthen me. It was only by his power, his grace and his mercy that I could overcome a life of pain and go forward as a new creature in him.

As I met with various pastors and attended chapel, I came to truly know the God of the Bible.

Each day I awoke filled with hope and eager to see what God had in store for me. No longer did I need to find my fulfillment in drugs, alcohol and other worldly things. I had found it in the one true source: Christ.

The next step to my healing was going to my family to ask for their forgiveness. "I know I've hurt you in the past, but I want to serve the Lord going forward. Please accept my apology. I'm a new person in Christ," I told each family member sincerely.

My parents, brothers and sisters were more than happy to oblige. They had been praying for me and wanted nothing more than to see me walking with the Lord. We rejoiced together at the miraculous healing God had performed in me.

My mother and I had a chance to talk about the resentment I'd harbored over the events with my brothers and sisters. I had buried this hurt deep down for years, allowing it to fester while avoiding healthy relationships with people. Through our tears, we worked out our feelings. I felt like a huge weight was lifted from my shoulders as we spoke. I was slowly becoming whole again.

After being in the program for a few weeks, I took a weeklong trip out of town to visit some friends. I was surprised at how eager I was to return to Freedom House. The pastors and peers there had become like family to me. Aside from the Lord, they were my primary source of encouragement and strength. I could hardly wait to get back and continue my healing journey.

When I returned from my trip, I learned that the golf course I had worked at for 10 years had shut down just a week after I entered Freedom House. I chuckled at the irony of the timing. "Clearly, you wanted me here right now," I told the Lord.

***

"Say, what are you going to do now?" Pastor Eric asked me one morning after chapel time. "When you graduate, got any plans up your sleeve?"

I shrugged. "I don't know. I could see myself doing missions down the line. There's so much I want to do. I want to help and serve others, to give back to the hurting world I once lived in. As long as I'm serving the Lord, that's all that matters."

"Well, I heard you might have a job here onsite," Pastor Eric replied, his eyes twinkling.

"Really?" I beamed. I had been working as a resident aide for the past few weeks at Freedom House and loved my job. I would have been happy working it forever, but I knew God had more in store for me. I had taken several soldering courses and enjoyed them immensely. This left the field wide open for what God wanted to do with my life.

"That's the rumor," he replied, smiling as he turned to walk away.

I smiled back. "Thank you, Lord," I whispered. "I don't know what you have in store for me down the road, but I know one thing for certain. You've given me a new hope and peace beyond what I ever could have imagined. You alone are the reason to wake up each morning. You are my peace, my joy, my everything. You have set me free."

As I walked back to my room, I realized I could hardly wait to get back in my Bible. Satan, I knew, would love nothing more than to see me fall flat on my face again. He had tried to entice me with drugs, the occult and everything else the world had to offer. But I had found true fulfillment in Christ alone, and nothing was more powerful than that!

A bird called outside my window, and I smiled at its song. The man who had gone tromping through the woods years ago flashed back to me for a moment. In the stillness of God's creation, I had found myself searching for something. All along, God had been right there, waiting for me. Now, my search was over. No longer would I spend my life wandering. I had found my resting place, my home.

I was right where I belonged, at last.

STONES OF SAND
The Story of Isaac Reeves
Written by Kevin Gill

You cast your stones with little class,
Forgetting that your house is glass —
With no regard for where they land,
In time your stones will turn to sand.
- Isaac Reeves

"Why are you always fighting with everybody?" my mother yelled. "I don't know what to make of it anymore! Everything I do, you're on my back!"

I ran my fingers through my short brown hair, trying to formulate an answer. I knew exactly why I was so difficult. In fact, I'd wanted to tell her for more than a year.

But I couldn't tell anybody. What had happened was beyond words. I could barely make myself think about it, but when I tried to concentrate on something else, my mind was invariably wrenched back to the dark hand around my mouth as I screamed and the dirty, humiliating agony that came from being violated by a stranger.

He'd been hiding behind a tree when I went to drop off some camping gear for a trip my friends and I had been planning. He streaked out and grabbed me before I could escape, covering my mouth with his hand.

"If you fight, I'll kill you."

But I did fight. I fought and screamed so hard my ears popped. But he was a full-grown adult, and I was only 12 years old.

One year later, I was still wrapped with guilt, self-condemnation and shame.

I was lashing out at everybody and growing increasingly depressed, and even as a 13 year old, I knew that if I didn't get help, I was going to crash.

So finally, I told my mother what had happened. She didn't know what to say.

Nobody did.

JOURNEY TOWARD FREEDOM

***

My mother enrolled me in counseling, but the sessions only managed to reopen the wound. We went over the same ground every session, like a surgeon painfully tearing stitches out to check and see if there was still a wound beneath. The pain continued to increase each time the protective scabs were torn off, until my spirit was virulently infected with angry bile. I was stained, and there was no way to wash myself clean.

My dreams grew worse. My mood darkened. The world sprouted eyes, which seemed to watch and judge me during every waking moment. I wanted to escape by any means I could. Food didn't fill the hunger in my soul, and I stayed overly slender, even for a 13 year old.

Inside, I was hurting so much that I couldn't contain it. I lashed out at every opportunity, trying to inflict my pain on others. My mother couldn't handle me so I moved to Rockford to live with my father.

But even though he kept me busy and instilled solid manly qualities into me, I only managed to discover one thing that numbed the pain and kept the nightmares at bay.

Drugs.

Crystal meth was one of the easiest to acquire in Rockford. It was generally easier for a minor to get than cigarettes and definitely easier than alcohol. It was like toilet paper — found nearly everywhere, but always in the grungiest place. And it flowed like pestilent water through the rusty pipelines of addicts and dealers.

EK, a gang with a strong presence throughout the prison system and across the country, had a solid presence in Rockford. Anyone with a few bucks and the right connection could get enough meth to stay loaded for two days. When I was high on meth, I could forget about the screaming pain in my soul. Even better, with enough meth, I could go six or seven days without sleep in one stretch. And when I finally slept, I was too exhausted to dream, which meant there were no nightmares. It seemed like the best of both worlds.

But meth cost money. I was too young to work, and my father didn't give me enough of an allowance to feed my chemical appetite.

So I looked for other ways to get my fix.

STONES OF SAND

***

My friend Denny invited me over to his house after school. He had an Xbox (and I didn't) so the invitation was like gold. We convened on his living room couch trying to cooperatively kill hordes of aliens. I didn't do very well; I simply hadn't had the chance to practice as much as he did. And something else kept distracting me, something sitting on the side sofa.

"I'll be right back," Denny said, tossing his Xbox controller onto the floor. He stood up and waddled into the bathroom, grimacing the whole way. His walk caused me to smirk — it was obvious he'd been holding off his urge to relieve himself until our game was over.

His mother's leather purse lay on the side sofa. It was begging to be opened like Pandora's Box, and I heard his mother rummaging through the kitchen down the hallway. I'd been eyeing the purse ever since I arrived at Denny's but hadn't seriously thought about stealing from it. But now that the opportunity presented itself, I sprang into action.

The Xbox's game noise covered my own, and my ears honed in on the sounds emanating from the kitchen. I knew that as long as the toilet hadn't flushed, I didn't have to worry about Denny. As for his mother, as long as I heard the clinking of dishes in the sink, I was safe from her catching me.

I quickly rummaged through the purse, taking out the wallet and snatching about half the money. I replaced the wallet and set the purse back on the couch exactly where it had been. The toilet flushed. The sink turned off. By the time my friend came back from the bathroom, I was sitting on the couch and playing Xbox as though I'd been there the whole time.

"I've got to run," his mother yelled from the kitchen. She strode into the living room and grabbed her purse. I felt a rush of heat through my head and neck.

Would she figure out what had happened? I focused on the TV screen, doing my best to ignore the twitch of my conscience. "You two be good. I'll be back in an hour."

"We will," Denny answered sharply, upset at the distraction from his game.

A few minutes after his mother left, I stood up. "I have to go."

"Okay. See you later."

JOURNEY TOWARD FREEDOM

I headed straight for one of the meth dealer's apartments. He was a member of EK, and I knew he'd be stocked. He was a manufacturer so it was cheaper to buy from him than a street dealer. The $340 I'd stolen bought me enough meth to last more than a week.

By the time I'd left his house, I was ramped up and spinning out of my head.

I'd only made it a couple blocks when I ran into Don. He was in his mid-20s and was a tattooed member of EK. Although I'd never hung out with him, I'd seen him dozens of times, and we'd exchanged small talk from time to time. His eyes and face were sunken, and his stringy hair was a sure sign that he was a hardcore meth addict.

"Hey, Isaac! What you up to, man?"

"Not much."

"You ever break into a car, man?"

I shook my head. It hadn't ever occurred to me.

"Come on, I'll show you. It's so easy, you wouldn't believe it." He pulled two butter knives and a screwdriver from his back pocket. "These are all you need to jack a stereo."

I was so high I didn't question a thing. I just followed along, enjoying the fact that someone wanted to teach me something. It was still broad daylight as we patrolled the streets, searching for a car that was parked off the beaten path. Nothing too new, nothing too old.

We headed right past a Neighborhood Watch sign and turned down a side street filled with potholes and an overgrown sidewalk. It didn't take long to find our target — a slightly used Toyota Corolla.

As we walked toward it, he explained some of the finer points of car theft.

"Twenty seconds. That's all it takes. Keep an eye out, all right?" He pulled a butter knife and the screwdriver out of his pocket, stuck the knife down the slit between the driver's side window and the door and jimmied the screwdriver into the lock. Five seconds later, the door popped open, and he slid into the driver's seat and used the two butter knives to pop the stereo out of its mount. He'd said he could do it in 20 seconds. I'd been counting, but I only got to 13.

"Good job, man," he congratulated me as we casually strode away. Even though I hadn't done anything, I felt like I'd been part of something special. Don was one of EK's "go-to guys" when it came to supplying their chop shop.

"Now you know how to do it. You can start bringing stereos over to us at the chop shop, and we'll give you money. What do ya think?"

"I'm down with that!"

He clasped me on the shoulder as if I was his younger brother. The warmth of acceptance spread through me, coupled with a revelation — I'd found another way to earn money for drugs. And it looked so easy that I couldn't see how anything could go wrong.

The next day, Denny didn't mention anything about his mother's missing money, but I resolved not to go over to his house again for a long time. I could get away with stealing from his mother once, but if I did it again, there would be no way to hide my tracks. And now that I knew how to break into cars, I had other options.

Stereos weren't the only things I took from cars. Most of the time I broke in, I took CDs, gloves or whatever else the owner had left inside. I tended to discard the things I stole, only keeping a select few things. It was more of a game to me than a way of making money. "Jockey Boxing" I called it.

I kept track of how long it took me to break in, steal things and get away. I was always looking for a way to cut corners, to shave some time, to beat my best. It was my version of NASCAR — and I was the top contender, the one everyone was gunning for. But nobody was fast enough to catch me.

I was becoming *The Speed Racer.*

It didn't take me long to ingratiate myself with EK. I started getting wholesale rates on drugs, and they also fenced my stolen goods. I learned how they operated and how they expanded. They took over a neighborhood one house at a time.

First, they'd rent someplace shabby on a rundown street, and they'd convert it into a meth lab. After they earned enough profit, they'd buy another house on the same street and convert it into a chop shop.

They were basically nonviolent, preferring to stick to car theft and a constant stream of profit that stemmed from dominating the local drug trade. If you wanted to become a member of EK, you had to prove yourself through carjacking, theft or whatever else they told you to do.

JOURNEY TOWARD FREEDOM

The other neighborhood gang was called Brood. The only things you needed to do in order to become a Brood was to be white, violent and racist. They used drugs but didn't manufacture them. They were the enforcers, making sure that the "wrong" elements stayed off their turf. If you weren't white and they found you anywhere near their turf, they'd beat you down hard and take everything you had. They robbed houses, smashed cars and were generally nasty. They called themselves the "Good People," but they behaved in the worst sort of manner. And they worked in conjunction with EK. The Broods secured an area and in return, EK provided them with drugs and acted like fences for the stuff they stole.

EK, Brood and the other gangs tended to hole up during most of the daylight hours. For the most part, the streets were safe and clean. There wasn't much violence, and the most common crimes were drug dealing and car theft. I felt pretty safe just about anywhere in the city while the sun was up.

But the cockroaches came out at night.

That's when most of the violence happened. And most of the junkies were either stoned or desperate for a fix.

***

"Did you see those wheels two blocks over? We need to chop that thing up!"

"Who wants to go?" Jay asked. He ran the chop shop, and nobody talked back to him. "What about you, Cowboy?"

"Send me after it," I boasted. "I'll get it!"

The three of them regarded me with a bit of skepticism. I was the only one in the room without the gang tattoo. And although they knew me and trusted me, I was still an outsider. But it didn't take Jay more than a few seconds to decide.

"Don't get caught, man. And whatever you do, *don't be followed.*"

The only difference between stealing my first car and stealing a radio was that I hotwired the car and drove away instead of leaving on foot. Nobody saw me, and I made it to the chop shop less than 10 minutes after I left.

"Frickin' sweet, Isaac!" Jay blurted, slapping me on the back. Don chimed in his congratulations. I felt like I was really part of something now. EK totally accepted me. And why wouldn't they? I was an asset — I made them money on a weekly basis.

After that heist, I couldn't wait to do the next one. I didn't do it for money — in fact, I never brought another car to the chop shop. I enjoyed the thrill of breaking in, hotwiring it and driving the car until its gas ran out.

Then, I'd find another car and drive it somewhere else. It was like I was living a real live version of "Grand Theft Auto" without all the violence. And if I needed somewhere to sleep, I'd drive a car off, park it somewhere the police wouldn't look right away and catch a nap in the backseat.

***

After I turned 16, my neighbor offered me a job, which I happily accepted. A stable income meant less chance getting caught dealing and guaranteed I'd never be short of meth.

Before long, I moved out of my father's house and rented an apartment with Flip and Cheeky, two other teenage junkies. Flip was scrawny and had all the features of a meth head — sunken eyes, missing teeth, even an eyebrow that would spasm at random times. Cheeky had cerebral palsy and couldn't use the left side of his body very well. I gave him a break on the rent to help him out, and he was thrilled to finally be living out of his parents' house. Between the three of us, we could easily afford the rent.

My new job consisted of cleaning carpets, which was the perfect occupation for a junkie. Most of the day's work happened in one to three hours with another two to three hours of driving to get to and from the job. I didn't have to drive so I could get high and stay up all night, then zone out during the drive and power my way through cleaning the carpets.

But while I thought I'd figured out the best way to live, things at my new apartment were taking a dangerous turn.

I'd just come back from a job when Flip greeted me at the door.

"Hey, come in here," he hissed excitedly. "I want to show you something."

I followed him into his room. There were several sunlamps and a couple rows of planters' pots. Each of the pots housed a budding marijuana plant.

"After these mature, I'll be able to pay all our rent just by dealing, man!" I'd never seen Flip smile this big before.

"This isn't gonna fly, man. I'm not going to jail because you're growing weed in my apartment."

"This stuff would pay our rent and a lot more," he argued. "Neither of us will have to work. It'll be party house, man!"

"We'll all go to jail!" I snapped back. "Get rid of it!"

The next day, both Flip and his plants were gone, leaving me to pick up his portion of the rent.

That Friday, I headed off to spend the weekend with a girl I'd met. We weren't compatible except for the fact that we were both lonely and empty. I actually felt a sense of freedom when I left Sunday evening to go back to my apartment.

But when I arrived home, my apartment was completely trashed. The sink was filled with beer cans and dirty dishes, the floor was littered with cigarettes and alcohol spills. The couch was stained, there was vomit in the toilet and Cheeky was sitting on the couch watching television.

"Hey," he said softly. His voice was raspy, and he looked like he'd been run over by a garbage truck. Black rings circled his eyes, his lips were puffy and his eyelids were barely open.

"You had a party? And you didn't even try to clean up the place?"

"It's just too much," he replied. "I can't do it."

"You could have at least tried! I mean, you trashed this place, and you want me to clean it up? What's wrong with you?"

"I can't do it."

"Well, you need to do a lot better than this! I can't believe this!"

I stormed into my room and slammed the door. There were a couple of beer cans on my bedspread, and I scattered them to the floor before flopping onto the grungy mattress.

"Clean this place up!" I screamed. I closed my eyes and went to sleep.

The next morning, the mess was still there, but Cheeky was gone.

Having been abandoned by both my roommates, I was only able to pay the rent for one more month. And when my next rent bill came, I ignored it for a while then took what few things I could and headed back to my dad's house.

My father let me stay there until I turned 18, then forced me to move into a new home — at least *I* called it home, but most people call it "the streets."

It was the lowest point of my life. I became angry. Angry at my father, angry at God, angry at everything and everybody. If nobody was willing to help me, I decided I'd do whatever I thought was necessary to help myself.

It didn't take long for me to figure out that sleeping in a bush wasn't the most comfortable thing to do. I'd already learned how to break into cars, so I started sleeping in backseats, doing my best to sneak out before the owners returned. Most of the time I was successful, but several times I was forced to make a hasty exit. I was never arrested, but I was yelled at and even had to sprint away on a couple occasions.

But the best, most comfortable setups I found were garage sales. They always had old furniture, including a couch that spilled from the garage onto the driveway or sometimes onto the lawn. By nightfall, everything the owners left outside was covered by a tarp. I'd wait until the owners went inside then sneak under the tarp and commandeer the couch. It was almost like camping. I was out of the weather, and unlike a backseat, I was able to stretch out comfortably.

I was low on cash, so I jacked a car radio and headed over to the EK chop shop. I traded the radio for a fair portion of meth and decided to check out the transition house to see if I could find a buyer.

The transition house or "Crack Shack," as we called it, was a gang-free zone. Race, color, gang affiliation — none of it mattered inside those tattered walls. Inside that one-bedroom rundown, flea-infested place, the only things that mattered was whether or not you had drugs or money to trade.

I needed cash for food, and although I stayed away from the Crack Shack as a general rule, it was the one place I knew I could go and make a quick deal.

Rusted cars were discarded on the dirt lawn, and cigarette butts littered the doorway like dandelions. I walked in without knocking and saw Tammy, the owner's daughter, huddling in the corner as several guys passed a weed pipe around. The only light came from thin cracks in a bent wall blind and the intermittent lighter flames that steamed up the drug "du jour."

"What's up, Tammy?" I asked. Her thin arms were crossed in front of her chest like she was trying to hug herself. She was trembling a bit, and I knew she was suffering from withdrawal. I was hurting and lonely so when she looked at me with hopeful eyes, I felt an empty warmth well up inside my chest — the illusion of acceptance, possibly even affection.

"Are you loaded, Isaac?" she asked. Her face turned into a desperately bright smile. "You got something to share with me?"

"Of course." I felt like a superhero as I sat down next to her and pulled out a small baggie of meth. It was my sharing bag. The bigger bag was meant for a richer house — one I could head into and break open once the weather got cold or wet. It would buy me two days of welcome while I partitioned it out. But like my relationship with Tammy, I was only welcome as long as the drugs were flowing.

We laid some meth out on a magazine cover and snorted it through a $5 bill. After Tammy had taken her third line, she laid her head on my shoulder and waited the three minutes for the meth to take effect. Her stringy blond hair fell across my chest, and I smelled the cigarette stink on her breath. It didn't bother me at all. My breath was the same.

For the next few hours, she pretended to care about me, which was more than anybody else did. But I was a bit worried. Tammy was Twitch's girl, or at least she had been the last I'd heard. And Twitch wasn't exactly known for holding back his temper.

But Twitch wasn't around right now, and I had the drugs, which meant I was temporarily the most important guy in the world — at least in her eyes. In this version of the world, the person with the most drugs was king. And drugs were more powerful than friendship, trust or anything else. To a junkie, drugs even ran thicker than blood.

Twitch was a high-up member in an all-black gang. His gang was as racist as the Aryans and just as violent. They only tolerated me in the transition house because it was a place of open commerce protected by the unwritten principle of drug-fueled greed. Here, drugs and money cut through gang lines faster than bullets could. Anyone could sell or get a fix — provided he behaved and had something worth trading.

I leaned against Tammy, letting the sick drug euphoria stream its way into our bodies. For a short while, I was able to relax — to imagine what life would be like with a steady girlfriend and enough money to live the high life. And even better, I imagined that the screaming pain in my soul would disappear and my emptiness would be filled.

But although I knew the meth would wear off, it dulled my pain enough for me to push its ugly head back into the cellar for a while.

My mind popped out of its haze as a dark shadow entered the room.

"You're stepping on toes, white boy!" Twitch yelled. "She's my girl!" He pulled a gun from his belt, and his whole body shook in anger. Adrenaline rushed into my brain, clearing my vision. I didn't like what I saw at all. Twitch's eyes looked like murder.

"I'm going to shoot you and put you in a garbage can! You think I'm going to let you take my girl?"

He was really spun, armed and angry — a definite bad combination.

I stood up and circled away. The house was far too small to run, and the only exit was the one Twitch was standing in. He had a gun and I didn't, which meant right now, he was completely in charge.

From behind me, someone's long black fingers wrapped around my throat. The fingers dug into my windpipe, and I could barely breathe. "Let's put him in my trunk," said the man who was choking me. Twitch moved toward me, slowly raising his gun.

"Back off!" A hardball voice stopped everyone in their tracks. Two Brood members had arrived just in the nick of time. The Broods were a violent white supremacist gang, and there was no way two Aryans were going to watch a couple of black men murder a white man, regardless of circumstances.

The rival gangs stared at each other like wolves ready to pounce. Finally, the tension broke.

"Next time," Twitch said, glaring at me. His eyes were thin and cold like knife blades. "You're living on borrowed time."

The fingers around my throat loosened, and I hurried away from the Crack Shack, shaking both from my drug high and the adrenaline-fueled fear of dying.

I made a decision.

It was time to get the heck out of Dodge.

JOURNEY TOWARD FREEDOM

***

Before I left, I made one hasty stop at my neighbor's house — the same one who'd given me the carpet cleaning job. His truck was gone, which meant he was out on a cleaning job. I'd heard him talk about how he liked to get stoned on weed, so I knew he'd have a stash somewhere in his house. Being a junkie, I knew to check his freezer. And I was dead on. Inside, covered by several bags of frozen vegetables, was a large bag of marijuana.

I snatched the bag and made a beeline for the EK lab. They valued the bag at $1,500 and traded me an equivalent amount of meth and cocaine. I got stoned with the dealer and left in a rush. Before Twitch and his gang could catch up with me, I stole a car and drove to Troutdale, a riverside stretch inside a 1,000-acre park.

Lots of hikers and campers frequented that park, but there were other denizens, as well. At any given time, roughly 30 homeless banded together like a caravan and bedded down for the night. But it was a caravan without wheels, going nowhere. Together, they managed to eke out a meager existence free from most of the traditional stresses of humanity.

I spent a lot of time getting drunk, getting high and writing. I really took a liking to poetry and expressing myself through the written word. Nobody down at the river seemed to care about poems unless they were drunk or I was giving them something. But every time I looked at the notebook and started scribbling my thoughts, I felt a sense of peace. Poem after poem, I wrote from the inspiration that was around me. Dirt, nature, grit and a twisted kind of freedom — free from most of the world's cares.

There were basically two types of homeless people at the riverside. There were the part-timers — people who spent half their time in the city, visiting shelters, getting clothes, going to soup kitchens, begging for money. They were easily recognizable from the second kind of homeless, the lifers. The part-timers had nice used clothing, and when they arrived at the river, they tended to look somewhat like hikers. They were generally stocked with a backpack of booze and food but were short in the bedding and kitchen department. But that "visitor" look wouldn't last for more than several days. Soon enough, the campfire smoke, cheap booze and grime would suck the new look right out of them. That's when they'd pick up and make another city run.

STONES OF SAND

The lifers, on the other hand, had continually tattered clothes. Many of them never bathed. And they were well stocked with things like portable TVs with extra batteries, pots, pans, full outdoor kitchens' worth of cooking utensils, tents, bedding, virtually everything it took to survive in semi-comfort. And every one of them had a pit bull. They took far better care of their dogs than they did themselves. Myself, I'd adopted a stray cat, which made me a bit of an oddity amongst them. I didn't quite fit in with the part-timers, and I didn't quite gel with the lifers. I started wondering which kind of homeless person I was more like until I looked at my cat. I'd fed it so well that it was fatter than any house cat I'd ever seen. In contrast, I was so thin that I could count each of my ribs. At 6'1", I weighed barely 130 pounds, which meant I was well on my way to becoming a lifer.

What bothered me the most was that I almost felt comfortable with that idea.

After several weeks of river life, I found myself sitting by the fire. My pen wrote fluidly, almost as if it had a life of its own:

> *You cast your stones with little class,*
> *Forgetting that your house is glass —*
> *With no regard for where they land,*
> *In time your stones will turn to sand.*

I stopped and read it several times. The poem made sense to me in a deep way. All around me, for as long as I could remember, people were constantly hurting others without any consideration for what their actions did. I was proud of that poem and thought about it many times each day.

But its meaning changed when I was struck with an intense realization — I'd actually written that poem for me. I'd forgotten that my house was glass. I was the one who'd cast my stones wherever I pleased, and now, all my stones had turned to sand. And the river's current was slowly eroding me away. I wondered how long I had left before I was gone completely.

***

My 19th birthday was fast approaching, and I decided to make a city run. I didn't know why, exactly. I was fairly comfortable at the river. I still had some drugs left, and as long as I had drugs to trade, I could get anything else I wanted. But I figured that someone might give me money for my birthday, and one thing was certain — I wouldn't get any special gifts if I stayed at Troutdale. So I picked up what few things I might want to keep and started my hike back to Rockford.

After getting a lifer to take care of my cat, I headed into the city. It was an entire week before my birthday, but I needed that much time to clean myself enough to be presentable. I smelled like cheap booze, old sweat and smoke. To keep the campfire going, we'd burn anything we could get our hands on from plastic bottles to Styrofoam and all sorts of random trash. We used plenty of wood, as well, but ironically, wood was hard to come by as the surrounding area had been picked clean year after year.

Each day, I washed myself with paper towels in public bathrooms, ridding myself of a bit more of the river stench. Then, after I'd reduced my body odor, I headed to a mission house and commandeered some new clothes. It took me all week for the booze and smoke smell to subside, but by the time I turned 19, I was ready to see my family again.

***

"Hi, Dad. I just thought I'd come by and say hello, since it's my birthday."

His expression couldn't hide his mixed emotions. He stumbled for the proper words. I was as uncomfortable as he was, but I didn't want to leave until he'd given me something.

"I just thought that maybe it would be nice to spend my birthday with you," I said quickly, "just in case you wanted to see me."

After a long pause, he reached into his pocket and took out his wallet.

"Here's $15," my father said. As he handed it to me, I saw his jaw clench. "Don't spend it on drugs. Okay? Don't spend it on drugs."

"I won't. Thanks."

I'd barely made it out of the yard when I found my feet pulling me to the nearest liquor store. I spent my father's gift on the biggest, cheapest bottle of vodka I could find. It was a plastic half-gallon bottle of something that was destined to make whoever drank it have an upset stomach and lose an inordinate number of brain cells, but I'd grown used to cheap rotgut at the river — it was all anybody down there ever drank.

Since I had very few places I could go, I headed over to an old friend's house, intending to share my drugs and crash there for a couple of days.

I knew I could get two days of shelter out of him; I'd done the same thing a dozen times in the past. He greeted me at the door of his double wide, and a familiar gleam flashed across his eyes. It was the gleam of a junkie who knew he was about to get rocked.

His girlfriend was less than happy to see me, but I ignored her, opened the vodka jug and put it on their rickety coffee table. Traces of cocaine dust lined the cracks in the table, and beer stains covered virtually every piece of carpet and furniture they had.

"Hey, could you go into the bedroom for a sec?" my friend asked me under his breath. "I need to sort things out with the ball and chain."

"Sure, man. No problem."

I strolled into his bedroom and plopped myself onto their mattress. While they argued, I lit up a cigarette and waited for my friend to pave the way for us to go on another bender.

A few minutes later, his girlfriend opened the bedroom door. As she did, I let out a lungful of cigarette smoke, and she freaked out. "He's blowing crack smoke in my face!" she screamed.

My friend rushed to the door. "It's not crack, it's just ..."

"I want him out of here!" she screamed.

"It's okay," I replied, trying to ease the tension. "I'll go right now."

I stood up and walked into the living room, detouring just enough to grab the vodka before heading out the door.

Outside, three police cars were waiting. Six policemen and a K-9 unit had surrounded the trailer. Someone must have seen me and reported it to the police.

"What's your name?" a policeman demanded. He, along with several others, had their guns drawn, pointed at the ground near my feet.

"Isaac Reeves," I replied.

"There's a warrant on you," the officer informed me after a quick check. His voice sounded like a drill sergeant's might. "You're under arrest. Are you going to fight us?"

"No, I'll come quietly," I assured them. I put the vodka down and raised my hands above my head. One of the officers wrenched my hands behind my back and cuffed my wrists.

***

After being arrested, I realized just how little support I had. Nobody came to visit me. Nobody would take my calls. It was like the world had spit me into a dark, bottomless chasm, and nobody could hear my cries for help. Or if they could, they ignored them, which only made the rejection hurt all the more.

My cellmate was a 21-year-old Vietnamese man who went by the name of Skids. All day, every day, he battered me with Bible verses that he read out loud. His choppy accent made the situation all the more annoying, but no matter what I did, he wouldn't give up.

"'The Lord is my rock, my fortress and my deliverer; my God is my rock, in whom I take refuge. He is my shield and the horn of my salvation, my stronghold!' You understand that, Isaac? That's Psalm 18:2." His voice echoed through our concrete prison cell, all the louder for the restricted space we shared.

It bounced through my skull the same way. "Skids, will you just shut up?"

He continued as if I hadn't spoken. "Oh! Here's one for you, Isaac. Deuteronomy 8:18: 'But remember the Lord your God, for it is he who gives you the ability to produce wealth, and so confirms his covenant, which he swore to your forefathers, as it is today.' That's what you need, Isaac. A covenant with the Lord!"

"Look, you're a convict, too, okay?" I retorted. "So quit being such a hypocrite, and shut the h*** up!"

But he didn't shut up. He kept reading out loud, growing in zeal with each Bible verse.

"When are you going to give your life to Jesus?"

"Shut up!"

"If you died right now, where would your soul go to?"

"I told you to shut the h*** up!"

A guard strolled up to my cell door. "You have a visitor."

The news shocked me. Nobody would want to visit someone like me. I couldn't even get anyone to take my phone calls.

The guard escorted me to the visitors' room where a chaplain sat, waiting to talk with me.

"Hi, Isaac," he stammered. "I know you didn't ask to see me, but your mother asked me to visit. So I prayed about it and decided to come see if you would like to talk to me."

It wasn't my habit to talk to preachers of any kind, but I didn't have anything better to do. And as I sat down, I realized that, strangely enough, I really did want to talk to him.

"Yeah. I'd appreciate that."

He smiled wearily and began to recite his testimony. "You see, I used to be a drug addict," the pastor explained. It felt like he was looking inside my soul — like he understood exactly what I was going through. "I've been in jail, I've slept on the streets and I've hurt people in ways I can never make right. I couldn't control what I did. Every decision I made was wrapped around one thing and one thing only — supporting my addictions."

As he spoke, tears started to pour out of his eyes. My own cheeks grew wet, and I did my best to wipe them dry, but I couldn't stop crying.

"You need to get yourself right with the Lord," the pastor said, sniffling. "It's the only chance you've got. He's the only one who can help you now. And if you don't trust in God, your life will only get worse from here. Why don't we get your life right with Jesus right now? We can pray together."

"Jesus," I prayed, my voice cracking with desperation. "Please help me. I'll give myself to you. But I need your help."

We cried together for more than half an hour before the pastor finally looked up and spoke.

"It's up to the Lord now," he said, wiping his cheeks clean. "We'll just have to see what Jesus does."

***

I kept looking for help from Jesus, hoping that he was truly as loving and compassionate as my cellmate and the pastor promised. But at my arraignment, nobody was willing to post bail for me. Not that I blamed them; I'd proven to be unreliable and a loose cannon on my best days, which meant that whatever bail money anybody put forward would likely be forfeited as soon as I made a run for it.

But at the last minute, a middle-aged couple arrived. Terry and Jamie McDonald were foster parents, and my brother had called them to see if they'd be willing to help.

"Are you here to post bail?" the judge asked them.

"Maybe, Your Honor," Terry replied slowly. "But first we'd like to talk to Isaac." Both he and his wife looked unsure, like they knew they were setting themselves up to be hurt.

"You can see him at 8 p.m.," the judge responded. "You'll have to wait until then."

8 p.m.? It was only 10 in the morning, which meant they'd have to wait a full 10 hours just to talk to me. Nobody would do that kind of thing for a stranger.

The judge brought his gavel down, and I knew my last chance at being bailed out had just been smashed into pieces.

I waited all evening, trepidation filling my chest. I kept praying that Jesus would help me, but truthfully, I didn't expect my prayers to be heard. I was a bad person. I'd done nothing but hurt people for the past several years. I deserved to be punished. What God would want to help someone like me?

But at 8 p.m., Terry and Jamie were still there. My heart fluttered when I saw them. I'd never met them, and all they knew about me was that I was a convict, a car thief, an addict, a drug dealer and I had been sentenced to 20 months on two felony counts: possession of a stolen vehicle and use of a stolen vehicle. Needless to say, my chance at a good first impression was already long gone.

"If you want our help," Terry explained, "there are four things you'll have to promise to do: Submit to us as one of our own children; work for us diligently; go to church with us every Sunday; and stay off drugs, which includes quitting cigarettes." Even though Terry's voice was soft, it carried a strength I couldn't ignore.

"I will," I replied with a weak voice. "I promise."

Two hours later, the McDonalds posted bail, and the judge remanded me into their custody. As he did, I broke down and bawled my eyes out. *Why would people be willing to risk so much on a total stranger?* It didn't make sense. *People didn't do that sort of thing, did they?* It was like the McDonalds were living in a completely different world than me — one whose rules and principles were completely opposite of everything I'd learned.

Food was everywhere at the McDonalds' house, and Jamie proved to be the best cook I could ever imagine. Under her care, I started gaining weight and losing my junkie traits. The circles around my eyes faded, and my skin took on a healthy color. Within a matter of weeks, I went from 130 pounds to 160 and started feeling healthy for the first time in years.

The McDonalds owned a highly successful plumbing company. Every day, Jamie packed a lunch for me, and Terry took me out to teach me the craft. He bought me a tool kit and started teaching me the trade.

By the time we came back home, I was exhausted. I stayed clean, went to church, quit smoking and did what they told me. And for the first time I could remember, I was happy. But I knew that this time would soon come to an end. With a 20-month sentence hanging over me, it was only a matter of time before I'd have to pay the piper.

I started looking for a way out. I'd learned that if I sought help on my own, there was a chance that the judge would reduce or suspend my sentence.

So I researched every drug rehab program in the state. The thought of being locked into a rehab program was more desirable than doing hard time in jail, but I didn't want to spend any more time in rehab than absolutely necessary. So I started calling the shortest programs possible.

None of the seven-month programs wanted me. Neither did the eight-month programs. So finally, after completely exhausting every other option, I picked up the phone and dialed the last possible option. It was a 12-month program called Freedom House.

After a face-to-face interview, they accepted me, so I packed my things and reluctantly opened a new 12-month chapter of my life.

***

The structure and discipline that the McDonalds had instilled in me helped me adjust to Freedom House's strict schedule, but it still took all of my willpower to make it through each day.

Everything was planned for us. Prayer time, devotions, Bible study, work, even our Sunday relaxation time was scheduled in advance.

This went against an entire lifetime of habits. I was used to doing what I wanted when I wanted and not having to answer to anybody.

So I started rebelling in whatever ways I could find — cutting corners, pretending to do my devotions and finishing my assignments with as little effort as possible. All I wanted to do was complete my time and hopefully get my prison sentence reduced.

Every morning, we prayed for a full half hour, starting at 7 a.m. sharp. But I wasn't exactly a *sit still* kind of person, so after a few days in the program, I stood up five minutes before prayer time was over and plopped myself onto a couch at the side of the prayer room. I hadn't been there 15 seconds when a senior student walked over and stood in front of me.

"Prayer time ends at 7:30, not 7:25," Ryan Smith admonished.

His voice pierced through me like fingernails on a chalkboard. I glared at him, but he was completely unmoved by my lashing stare.

"It's not 7:30 yet," he continued. "You need to keep praying."

We locked eyes. There was no way I was going to let some Jesus freak tell me what to do. I was too good for that. And I wasn't here to pray, I was here to reduce my prison sentence.

Ryan's gaze didn't flicker even for a moment.

It took two minutes for me to break, but in the end, he wrung another three minutes of prayer out of me. As soon as the clock struck 7:30, I was *done.*

The next morning, I quit praying at 7:25 again. I'd spent all night psyching myself up for my next *samurai eye battle.* There was no way I'd let the annoying senior student beat me again. Not in this lifetime.

"Prayer time ends at 7:30," Ryan said with a grating voice, "not 7:25."

This time I was ready. I whipped my head around, staring him down with all the cold, hard anger I could muster. We locked eyes.

This time, he got four minutes of prayer out of me. But as I defiantly clasped my hands together and bowed my head, I resolved to do better next time.

The following morning, I decided that it simply wasn't worth hearing Ryan's voice again, so I prayed for the entire 30 minutes. And the next day, I did the same.

STONES OF SAND

***

"Tomorrow, we're going to a men's retreat," a counselor announced. "So make sure to pack two days' worth of clothes and your Bible."

The thought of spending two days with men worshiping the Lord was as exciting to me as watching a gallon of water evaporate. It was hard enough doing my devotions (which I didn't believe in) and listening to other peoples' testimonies. The last thing I needed was to be locked in a camp with a bunch of broken druggies. All I wanted to do was finish my time at Freedom House and hopefully convince my judge to reduce my sentence.

I thought about pretending to be sick so I wouldn't have to go, but I decided that it would be best if I played along so I could convince my counselors to give me good recommendations once my time here was up.

The retreat started with a worship session at 5 p.m. sharp. As the music played and people around me began to sing praises, my crossed arms slowly loosened until my hands fell to my sides. Little by little, my defiance was ground away until I found one of my hands in the air and I was praying and doing my best to sing along. I didn't know the melodies or words of the songs, but the lyrics I sang were poems that sprang spontaneously from deep inside of me. And I realized that I was praising the Lord.

It felt right.

A boulder of tension formed in my torso until I could barely breathe. Then, in a flash of light, a hammer struck my chest. The hammer was invisible, but I felt it as clearly as if it were real. Pain lanced through my ribs, and something broke inside my heart. My body turned hot, and the pain slowly faded. My mind began to clear, and I broke down in tears.

It felt like I was being cleansed — my guilt washed away. Guilt, shame, self-condemnation, judgment — they all left through my tears. The bitter coil of emotions I'd been harboring since I was assaulted at age 12 started to unwind, and the tension in my spirit dissipated. I hadn't known how much pain I was in until I felt it lifted from me, and for the first time in years, I was able to think of things other than myself. I started actually hearing what people were saying about God. A cloak of deafness had been taken from my ears.

The next day, the man I disliked the most invited me on a hike through the woods. Ryan Smith led me off the trail, and we trudged through mud and dense foliage that no other animal had ever pushed through. Two hours later, we were both covered with mud, scratches, welts and bug bites.

It was the most fun I'd had in years.

During the walk, we had plenty of time to talk and get to know each other. "You have to submit your will to God," Ryan explained. "That's why I've been so hard on you. You've been trying to do things your way, but the only way to live is to do things God's way. Believe me, I've been where you are, and I know exactly what it's like. If you're 99 percent trustworthy, you're 100 percent untrustworthy. If you're 99 percent disciplined, you're 100 percent undisciplined. That one percent is an open floodgate in your spirit for addictions to work their way back in.

"Your mentors — they're not being tough on you just because they're mean or want to hurt you. They care about you and want you to succeed because all of us know what it's like to hit rock bottom. I used to do drugs every chance I could get because it had become the only thing I knew how to do. But now, I've learned how to be disciplined. That's what I want you to learn. If you leave a single crack in your foundation, you'll crumble."

Everything he said felt like a hammer hitting a nail on the head. He didn't put up with nonsense because he lived the same standard he expected from others. I finally understood why he was so hard on me.

He wanted me to win. And he was a living example of God's transformation. And by the time we returned to the retreat area, Ryan Smith had become one of the people I respected most in my life.

During the rest of the retreat, I learned the spiritual truths behind financial stability, leadership, commitment, bravery and relationships. My spirit was being sharpened on a grinding stone. And since my ears were no longer deafened with the devil's lies, I was able to hear and finally understand what I was being taught.

When I came back from the retreat, I started taking what I heard seriously. It finally sunk in. I saw how messed up my mind had become, how wounded my spirit was. And I realized how broken I'd become. That was why I'd fallen so far down before letting God pick me back up.

STONES OF SAND

The McDonalds visited me every second week and were pleased with the progress I was making.

"Isaac," Terry said during one of our visits, "there's something I've wanted to tell you. Jamie and I have tried to help three other people in the same way we've helped you. And all three of them disappointed us. They stole things, were rude and unappreciative. In fact, we'd decided never to open up our home like that again, but God put it on my heart to try just one more time. We were afraid you'd disappoint us, but I wanted to tell you — I'm so proud of you, Isaac. Everything we've done for you was more than worth it."

I bawled my eyes out. It was just like I cried when the McDonalds bailed me out. But these tears weren't ones of desperate self-condemnation and grief; they were born of unconditional love. Jesus *had* answered my prayers. The McDonalds' love had truly saved me, and I realized that no matter what I did, I couldn't bear the thought of letting them down.

***

When I was a junkie, I'd always believed that blood ran thicker than money, but drugs ran thicker than blood. I'd seen friends and families fall apart over drugs. I'd seen people betray each other — lie, cheat and steal — and I'd made every decision with one thing in mind: to score my next fix. But now, thanks to the people who were willing to step out in faith and reach out to me one final time, I'd learned that something was stronger and more powerful than anything else.

Love.

I'd always heard that it takes a lot longer to build something than to tear it down. And while I assumed that idea referred to good works, I didn't understand that the devil's works were even more fragile than God's. It had taken me years to hurt my family and hit rock bottom. But within three months at Freedom House, my relationship with my family was restored. They started trusting me again and going out of their way to let me know they believed in me. In three short months, I realized how much my actions had hurt people — from the people who had trouble because I'd stolen their cars, to the junkies who had relied on me to feed their addictions. I wanted to reach out to all of them and make things right.

But there was no way I could ever go back and heal the things I'd done. Some things were simply out of my control. Some things could only be sorted out by God.

And so I continue to pray for the ones I hurt. I pray that God will heal them like he's healing me. And I pray that God will give me the chance to make things right, however I can.

> *You cast your stones with little class,*
> *Forgetting that your house is glass —*
> *With no regard for where they land,*
> *In time your stones will turn to sand.*

My worldly stones had turned to sand. But God is helping me pack that sand into the right foundation so my house won't shift and shatter every time the storms strike my life. And although I know the hard times aren't over, I finally understand that Jesus will see me through anything as long as I continue to seek him with every fiber of my being.

As I look back over all the crazy things I've been through, it's obvious that I'm alive only because of God's grace, which is why I know he'll always be there protecting me, lifting me up and guiding my steps with his undying grace. And I can't wait to see the other miracles God has planned for me. Because I know for certain that whatever the future holds, I'll always have a special place in God's heart, and he'll always have the *most* special place in mine.

SHORT CIRCUIT
The Story of Bill White
Written by Kevin Gill

The bus ride from Freedom House in Portland, Oregon, to McCall, Idaho, lasted 23 hours, and by the time I arrived at the catering area, I was completely beat. I hadn't slept a lick, being more concerned with protecting my luggage from getting stolen than catching some shuteye. So I had a lot of time to ponder my life — something I hadn't done in months, at least not sober.

I was half-black, half-Asian with naturally straight hair — a minority among minorities. People often had trouble placing me, and this bus ride was no different. Several people stared at me, and I wondered if they were curious about my ethnicity or were scoping me out to steal my luggage.

As I cradled my suitcase under my arm and tried to get comfortable on the stiff bus seat, my thoughts drifted back to Alaska when I'd first sought out help for my drug addictions.

***

"Bill," my counselor had explained with a wavering voice, "you're not as bad off as you think. You're holding down a job and paying your bills — you don't need inpatient care."

Translation: Unless you have $25,000 on hand, or get yourself into a lot of trouble, you're stuck with our economy rehab program. Outpatient only. And there's no way I could come up with that kind of money.

I'd been working at an inventory company, but I hadn't realized the work was seasonal, and after summer, my hours had been cut back drastically. I'd gone from full-time to barely making $150 a week.

That wasn't nearly enough to pay my bills, so I'd ended up living in a homeless shelter and trying to work my way back from there. I had barely a penny to my name. And the few pennies I *had* saved had gone into feeding my drug habit.

He was right — I wasn't as bad off as I thought. I was worse. And now, I was as desperate as I'd ever been in my entire life.

JOURNEY TOWARD FREEDOM

I leaned over the desk and stared him dead in the eye. I spoke through clenched teeth. "Do I need to come across this desk and do something we'll both regret in order to get help?"

The counselor shrank back a bit. I was nearly five inches taller than him, muscular, desperate, trained in karate and after all the stress I'd been through, my eyes must've looked like firecrackers ready to explode.

"There's nothing I can do," he stammered apologetically. His blond beard quivered slightly as his jaw shook with tension. "You're an addict, but you're still functional. I can only admit the hard cases."

If he had known exactly how much of a hard case I was, he would've let me in right away. Ever since I was a kid, people called me "knucklehead," and while that tag had bothered me initially, over the years it grew into a mark of pride. To me, "knucklehead" meant *indomitable* — strong, unconquerable, resolute. And that was my problem. Whenever I put my mind to something, I always followed it through. That's why my rampant drug use hadn't crashed me earlier. Even though I used as many drugs as a hard-core junkie, I was able to stay disciplined in areas that other junkies let fall. I paid my bills, I never missed work (no matter how much I was suffering) and I pushed through the pain of withdrawal when others would've curled up in their beds and let the world crash down around them.

Yes, I was a knucklehead all right — both in the good and bad sense of the word. And I knew that if I didn't get help soon, I'd end up back on the street, in jail or dead. No matter how much I wanted to change, as long as I was in the same environment with the same people, there was no way to break free from my downward spiral. I'd tried to clean up more times than I could count, but every time, I'd run into an old acquaintance who'd offer me some marijuana, cocaine or crack, and I'd fall back into my old habits.

The last 30 years had been like living under a constant storm. Between prison, trials and drugs, I'd barely had time to keep my head straight. Even the happy times were tainted by a foreboding darkness as if thunderclouds were always hovering ominously overhead, ready to loose a cascade of lightning into my life.

They say that lightning never strikes the same place twice, but that's not true. There are places that have been struck by lightning hundreds if not thousands of times. Their polarity is such that whenever a storm comes anywhere near them, they pull lightning from the sky, smiting themselves again. My drug use had become the same sort of conduit, and no matter how hard I worked at keeping my life together, the storms continued to grow closer until I could almost feel the next bolt of lightning straining to strike.

My stubbornness worked both ways — it got me into trouble, but when I decided to do something, I never backed down. After countless phone calls, I realized that there wasn't anywhere in Alaska that could give me the help I needed. So I started looking into programs in the continental United States. One after the next, I eliminated dozens of treatment centers. They were either too expensive, already full, only took insurance or simply wouldn't accept people from other states. Finally, I asked Pastor Pauline, my mother's pastor and good friend, for help. Pastor Pauline was running the Halfway House for women, where my ex-wife, Ladean, had been placed. She recommended a center called Freedom House.

I picked up the phone one more time, and as my fingers dialed the long distance number, I prayed this would be the last call I'd need to make.

"We're a relatively new program," the head of Freedom House informed me over the phone. His name was Jim, and I could tell by his voice that he was a heartfelt man, deeply committed to his work. "But we'll make room for you. The only thing is that you'll have to come up with your own transportation here and be completely serious about completing the program. This is a completely voluntary yearlong discipleship program. The entire focus is on faith-based Christian character development, and it takes a lot of discipline to see it through to the end."

"Oh, I'm serious," I assured him. "After everything I've been through, I need to change, no doubt about it. I'm willing to do whatever it takes to get my life straight — if I don't, I'll end up dead. I already know that."

"Well, it costs $450 to enroll, and you'll need to find your own transportation."

That amount of money was out of my reach. I barely had $50 to my name and was living in a homeless shelter. But Pastor Pauline was serious about getting me help.

"I'll pay your way," she said. "But I want you to promise me that you'll graduate. I don't want my money and trust to be wasted."

"I'll graduate," I assured her with the same conviction I'd had when I spoke with Jim. I'd never done anything to deserve this kind of charity, and the idea that someone would go out on a limb like this for me warmed my heart and bolstered my resolve to stay clean. Pastor Pauline talked to several people in the congregation about my airfare, and one of them bought me a plane ticket with his frequent flyer miles. I never was one to ask for much or expect to be given anything, so I barely knew how to thank the people who helped me. But I did my best, and before I knew it, I was on an airplane flying across Canada — destination Freedom House.

Freedom House was a relatively new program. It was completely voluntary and lasted for an entire year, which in my view was a good thing. It had taken me a long time to get myself into this mess and would take time to unlearn my bad habits. Besides, I'd spent years in jail, and the thought of living in a place without bars seemed like a walk in the park. Still, the thought of being subjected to an entire year of religious brainwashing didn't appeal to my defiant nature. But this was the only program that would take me and didn't cost an arm and a leg, so I decided to go and see what the program could do for me.

But when I arrived, the building was eerily quiet.

"Everyone is out at Fire Camp," Lynn explained. As Freedom House's executive assistant, she'd remained behind to greet me and help me get enrolled into the program. "They're supporting firefighters in McCall, Idaho. Tomorrow, you'll be taking a bus to join them."

She gave me a brief tour. Freedom House was located primarily on the second floor of a square three-story building. It took up half of that floor and part of the third floor, as well. There was a general-purpose room that was used for everything from eating to movies. The second floor consisted of classrooms and dorm rooms, and the interior of the building sported a courtyard with a variety of plants.

It reminded me of a hotel. The beige exterior was ringed with covered walkways and metal staircases. The interior was a variety of colors from beige to faded red, with several of the rooms being covered in patterned wallpaper. Overall, the facilities weren't run down, but it was obvious that there was room for work to be done.

Still, it was a comfortable environment, and after finishing the tour, I was glad I'd chosen to enter the program.

That night, with thoughts of hope cascading through my mind, I slept more soundly than I had in years.

***

On the other side of the aisle and a couple seats back, a crusty alcoholic cradled an old radio on his lap. The volume was low, but loud enough for me to barely make out singer Berry John's voice over the dull roar of the bus engine.

Disaster's getting closer every time we meet
Goin' 90 miles an hour down a dead end street
Goin' 90 miles an hour down a dead end street

The words were painfully apt. And besides the fact that the Greyhound was traveling about half that fast, I couldn't help but wonder if that song had come on just to remind me of what kind of life I was trying to leave behind.

Outside, the weather took a dark turn, and raindrops started to patter on the bus windows. Thunder rumbled across the sky, and a moment later, the bus drove into a wall of water. The driver turned the windshield wipers on full blast and, as lightning lit the cascading sky, it gave me an odd sense of comfort. As a certified electrician, I saw lightning as a dangerous ally.

There's nothing to fear about electricity. If you're unfortunate enough to become a conduit, there's nothing you can do. Everything happens in less than the blink of an eye. One moment, you're resetting fuses or touching what should be a dead wire. The next, you're flying through the air, body locked up like you're made of bricks. Before you know what happened, it's already over. If it kills you, you wouldn't even know it, and if you live, there's no reason to worry. So you do your best to be careful and hope the people you're working with are doing their jobs right.

And in the same way you can't determine where lightning strikes, you can't prevent other people from making mistakes. And when you're jolted, it's almost always due to forces outside your control.

JOURNEY TOWARD FREEDOM

Lightning lanced through the sky, and thunder drummed several seconds later. As the rumbles faded into the distance, I pondered just what had happened to short circuit my own life.

Unconsciously, my eyes found their way to my disfigured left wrist. Just then, lightning flashed outside the bus window, and thunder boomed so closely that it sounded like a gunshot ...

***

The paramedic wrapped my left hand in a plastic bag, preserving what little flesh was left. I barely felt anything — adrenaline and endorphins were rushing though my system, doing their best to dull the pain and keep me on my feet. My fingers looked like white straws dangling from a bloody balloon at the end of my wrist. The rifle bullet had torn through my hand, rending virtually everything away down to the joints and ligaments.

As the paramedic finished wrapping my hand, a police officer walked up with a notepad and started questioning me.

"What instigated the confrontation?"

"He hit my car," I replied, dazed. I'd already answered the same question a half dozen times and was in no mood to keep repeating myself. Each time I had to recount what had occurred, I felt more knuckleheaded than before.

"And what happened after that?"

"He sped away. I followed him to this house."

The officer jotted down some notes. "And then?"

"I already told you —"

"Just answer the question, please."

The paramedic interrupted him. "We have to get him to a hospital."

The officer followed us toward the ambulance and continued his questioning as the paramedic opened the rear doors. "You said you were knocking on a door across the street from where he parked his car when —"

"— he came at me from behind, pointing the rifle at my head. I whirled and pushed the barrel away, but he fired and the bullet went through my hand."

In the distance, I saw two policemen securing my assailant in the back of a cruiser. He was babbling and glancing around nervously with his bloodshot and dilated eyes.

SHORT CIRCUIT

The paramedic escorted me into the back of the ambulance and shut the door, cutting off the remainder of the officer's questioning.

As the cruiser and ambulance both pulled away, I grimaced in regret. I'd known it was a mistake to chase him down. He'd been driving erratically the entire time, and I'd guessed he was on some sort of drug. But knucklehead that I was, I didn't want to let him get away. So the "hit and run" had turned into an attempted homicide, and as a memento, I suffered a disfigurement that would never heal.

But I was more angry with God than myself.

How could you let this happen to me? my spirit wailed. *Lord, you're supposed to protect me!*

My mother was a stern churchgoing woman, and I'd been brought up believing that Jesus was my Lord and Savior. So having been shot cast a tremendous amount of doubt on my faith. Even more than a physical injury, it was an injury in my belief that God truly cared about me. And from that day forward, I quietly made a vow.

If this is how he let my life unfold, I didn't need him anymore.

It took 18 months and 15 surgeries before my hand was somewhat operational again. And by the time I was off the pain medication, I'd become a full-time drug addict. Prescription drugs were my escape from the painful reality of where my bullheadedness had taken me. When I was sober, my head was constantly swarmed with thoughts of how stupid I'd been. If only I'd kept my temper in check, I'd still have my hand intact. But no matter how much I dwelt on the situation, there was no way to change any of it. So the painkillers the doctors prescribed to help me through my surgeries became the staple I used to forget.

***

As the bus engine hummed, I was pulled out of my memories. My eyes were locked on my reconstructed hand. It was three inches shorter than the other, and the bones were fused into my wrist so I could barely turn it at all. I flexed the fingers — my thumb didn't move; its ligaments were too badly injured to reattach. I winced as it came into focus, shocked at how much it still affected me. Yes, this had been the incident that first caused my life to short circuit. It's amazing how much your physical state can change your life. Before my injury, I'd been on the straight and narrow — training in martial arts every day, athletic, clean, sober, filled with hope. But the trauma done to my body had translated to my mind and sense of identity. I'd never felt whole again.

The bus slowed down and turned into a parking lot. "End of the line," the driver announced as he pulled to a halt. I pushed the memories aside and stood up, stretching.

When I stepped off the bus, my legs felt like rubber and my spirit like a circuit box ready to blow all its fuses at once. My body was running on too little voltage when Jim, the head of Freedom House, greeted me.

"Glad to see you made it," he said with a quick handshake. He could tell I was exhausted, so he kept things short. He asked about my bus ride and my plane trip from Alaska, and he did his best to make me feel welcome. After I explained how I hadn't slept, he set me up in a new tent as all of the staff and students were camped in tents. He then told me to rest up for a day before joining the other members of Freedom House working in food service as they catered to the firefighters. I gladly took him up on his offer and after a quick shower, settled into bed.

The tent was a different experience than I was expecting after such a trip, but everything necessary was there and provided for — and I mean everything. It was obvious that this team had done this type of work out in the forest and fields many times before. A nice cot, a foam mattress and a new sleeping bag. It was different for sure but, thankfully, I was truly comfortable — and besides, the mattress wasn't bolted into some wall, and there were no locked bars on the doors or windows. It was a tremendous step up from the prison cells I'd been forced to inhabit.

Lying there, staring at the fabric above my head, I couldn't help but remember the years I'd been locked up. That was another life — one on which I didn't care to dwell — but it was impossible to bury those memories deeply enough to forget. And I didn't see how it would do me any good to pretend to be anything other than what I was — a man who'd done 10 years of hard time, a beaten down, 51-year-old, knuckleheaded junkie with no prospects and a pattern of bad habits that lead nowhere but down.

When I opened my eyes, I realized I'd fallen asleep. The room was spinning from my exhaustion, and it took me several minutes to force myself to sit up. I washed up and changed into my work clothes then headed back to find Jim. He was already on the food line helping a dozen students make portable breakfasts.

"This is Port-A-Pit," Jim explained. "They're a company that supplies food for a wide variety of events — firemen containing forest blazes, athletic events, you name it. This time, they're supplying a biking event where nearly 1,200 bikers ride around most of Oregon."

"Sounds good to me," I replied. "I like to work, anyway."

After a brief orientation, we put together 1,200 sandwiches that first day, and the hours disappeared like the blowing wind. Outside, it was overcast and a bit drizzly, but we worked inside of portable trailers so the only indication we had of the weather was a permeating dampness that preceded an inevitable rain. Once in awhile, I saw the Port-A-Pit supervisor glancing at me but didn't think much of it. I was used to being watched after spending so many years in lockdown.

At the end of the day, the Port-A-Pit supervisor approached me.

"Nobody works as hard as you do," he observed. "What line of work do you come from, anyway?"

"I was an electrician."

"No kidding? You know, we've got a lot of things that could use some fixing. You think you could take a look at some of them?"

"Sure."

"How about you come talk to me tomorrow morning. Good job today."

His words caused odd, warm tingles to arc up my spine, and I stood for a second, trying to figure out how to react. I wasn't used to being complimented. Positive reinforcement was a type of energy that I wasn't wired to take.

"Thanks," I stammered, then headed off to join the rest of the students.

We packed everything up and drove to the next stopping point, after which I gratefully retired to bed.

The next day, we woke up early in order to get an early start making breakfast for the riders.

The supervisor led me to an industrial coffee pot in their portable trailer-mounted kitchen. "This thing hasn't worked in months. I was about ready to pitch it. You think you might be able to do something with it?"

"I can try."

I fiddled with it for about 10 minutes before finding a wire with a short. Five minutes after that, the smell of freshly brewing coffee filled the kitchen as the pot pushed hot water through some grocery store grounds.

"That was fast," the supervisor said with a smile. "I can smell that coffee all the way out to the line. You up for some more work?"

"Of course," I answered, shrugging.

Light fixtures, switches, broken appliances — he brought me to one broken thing after another, and I spent the rest of the day fixing old wires that should have been replaced years ago.

I alternated the ensuing week making sandwiches, doing custodial work and fixing whatever odd pieces of equipment that needed some care. And before I knew it, I was back in the maxi van heading back to Freedom House, this time surrounded by familiar faces and no longer worrying about getting my bags stolen.

In certain areas of my life, discipline had never been a problem, but in other areas, it was my Achilles heel. If I was supposed to be somewhere at a certain time, I was there. Wake up at 4:30 a.m., no problem. Work until a job is done — absolutely. But asking me to take correction or submit to authority was like telling an overloaded fuse not to blow. I had my own version of how things should be done, and I wasn't about to let anyone else tell me what to do.

So adapting to Freedom House's strict schedule was harder than I'd expected. Even though I'd been eased into the program, having had a chance to work on the food line before getting oriented, actually submitting to the Freedom House curriculum rubbed me the wrong way. Everywhere I went, someone accompanied me, watching my every move. They called this an "accountability partner," but I called it downright annoying. I was more than 50 years old and besides my time in lockup, I'd barely had to account to anybody for anything. And every time someone corrected me, I felt like a kid being scolded by my mother. Now they may have been motivated by love, but I wasn't in the mood to take it that way.

SHORT CIRCUIT

My reputation as an electrician caught up to me, and before long, Jim came to talk to me. "There's a lot of electrical work that needs to get done around the campus here. God gave you a special gift in that area — do you think you'd mind helping us out?"

"Not at all. It'll be nice to do something I'm good at."

To say there was a lot of work was an understatement. Freedom House ran as a faith-based organization — "faith-based" meaning "barely getting by." They'd recently moved into the facilities, which had been neglected for years before Jim started the refurbishment. Nearly one-third of the wires were faulty, and although they weren't particularly dangerous, they needed extensive work before they'd become functional.

So my duties at Freedom House consisted mainly of updating and fixing the wiring. But I didn't realize that the most important rewiring was happening within my own mind, heart and soul. For each machine, circuit or fuse that I replaced, another was fixed inside me. My attitude improved, I started getting hope back and I started seeing my injured hand differently — as a conduit for God to enter my life.

***

After two months, I graduated from Level 1. The biggest change between Level 1 and Level 2 was that I no longer needed an accountability partner. This meant I had some time to myself in which I could read, study and pray. At first, the extra freedom was uplifting, but before too long, it opened up a series of new challenges, the biggest of them being the temptation to revert to my old mindset.

When you're accountable to somebody, you're almost like brothers. You look after one another, making sure you stay on the right track and picking each other up when you stumble. But now that I was on my own, it was harder to stay focused. They say that runners always go faster when they've got someone else with whom to run. They'll push through all sorts of cramps, fatigue and pain in order to keep up with each other. And that's how I felt. Once I had time on my own, I didn't push myself as hard, and before long, I'd let negative thoughts slip into my mind, and my progress began to short circuit again.

Jim rarely disciplined the students, but when he did, there was no way to hide. He strode into our classroom during an instruction session, jaw bulging.

"Some of you," he said with a raised voice, "think the rules don't apply to you. You're allowed one cup of coffee in the morning, but you're having three or four. You're supposed to memorize your proverbs, but all you're doing is staring at your books, not reading a thing. How do you expect to change if you're not putting in any effort?"

His words were honest, but being yelled at was a definite hot spot for me. I started to speak, but he cut me off, his voice rising to a yelling tone. "You think you can just do whatever you want and God will ignore your rebellion? What are you here for? To waste your time?"

I couldn't take it anymore. I didn't put up with anybody yelling at me for any reason.

To h*** with this, I thought, slamming my Bible shut. *If these people aren't going to treat me like I deserve, who needs them!* After all, I wasn't a kid, I was a grown adult! And there was no way I'd let myself be talked to that way, especially by a younger man.

I stood up and stormed out of the classroom, but Jim blocked my path.

"Where do you think you're going?" he demanded.

"Get out of my face!" I yelled back and pushed my way past him.

I headed to my room where I started packing my few things. It took me all of 10 minutes to bundle up everything I owned in the world. I hoisted my suitcase off the bare mattress and strode toward the door.

But as I reached out to turn off the light, my mother's voice cut through me seemingly from nowhere. *Boy, do you think this is what I want for you?*

Her words hit me like she was right there in front of me, gazing at me with her stern, loving eyes. Even from beyond the grave, her love still touched me.

"No, Mom," I answered quietly.

A few moments later, Jim arrived. "Are you ready to talk yet?" he asked.

"I'm sorry," I replied. "I want to make it through."

"I want you to make it, Bill. That's why I'm hard on you guys.

If you can't learn to submit to the authority of a man, how are you supposed to submit to God's authority?"

My head hung on its own accord. Blowing up was what got me in trouble in the first place. If I'd kept my temper in check, I never would have gotten my hand shot. I was supposed to be a grown man — disciplined, not behaving as a child. And although I was loathe to admit it, I knew that Jim was right. Suddenly, my mind cleared up as if the Holy Spirit of common sense came over me. I realized that if I left the program, I'd end up worse off than I'd ever been. And I'd promised both Pastor Pauline and Jim that I'd finish the program. I had to be a man of my word — it was all I had left.

"I apologize."

Jim patted me on the shoulder. "We're on your side, Bill. I'm glad you're staying." Then, after praying with me, he left my room.

And after a long, ashamed pause, I started unpacking.

From that day forward, I truly committed to finishing the program. No matter what it took, I'd finish the year out. Otherwise, why did I waste all that time and effort to get my life right if I was simply going to walk away from the only place that could help me?

I unpacked the last of my few belongings then shut off the light in my room. As the switch flipped off, it felt like I'd just shut off the current to my old life. And in the darkness, as I walked to my bed and into an unknown future, the only light I could see was the one that God was placing in my soul.

The next few mornings, I prayed in earnest and did my best to memorize proverbs. Then, after breakfast, we gathered for a worship service and classroom instruction. In the afternoon, I fixed electrical problems. In the evening, I worked on my homework assignments. Little by little, I started getting the facilities up to speed. And more importantly, I started getting my own life together.

Freedom House didn't focus on drug rehabilitation. It focused on God and building Christian character, the theory being that once your mind and heart were filled with God, the other things would all fall into place.

That evening, Jim asked me to look at a building in which the lights were flickering. I poked around several places, checking everything from the circuit breaker to the wiring. Several of the wires had tiny teeth marks on them, and I suspected that the problem in the building was caused by the same thing.

JOURNEY TOWARD FREEDOM

It took me about 30 minutes to find the culprit — a frayed main wire that was close to a metal pipe. I pulled out a sensor and checked the connection. Sure enough, I'd found the short.

"I think I found the problem," I explained. "Something chewed through the wires, and some of the electricity is arcing over to this pipe. That's why the lights are flickering — the current is bleeding away. We'll have to cut the power back for me to fix it."

I used my reconstructed hand to hold things in place, but it had limited mobility, so most of the heavy work was done with my right hand. Like always, doing physical labor was a form of meditation, and as I spliced a new wire into the socket, my mind drifted back to a different time.

My mother was a devout Christian for as long as I could remember, and it was she who led me to Jesus when I was younger. And she wasn't the kind of lady to hide her feelings, so it didn't take too long after my final surgery for her to sit me down for an intensive heart-to-heart conversation.

"You are behaving like a sick little baby," she said. "I raised you better than that! These things you're into — boy, are you going to just throw your whole life away?"

Her scolding tone brought forth my defiant nature.

"How could God let this happen to me?" I demanded.

"Boy, I am sick and tired of this pity party! God didn't shoot you, a man shot you, so get over it!"

Those words echoed through my memories as I finished splicing the wire. And as I flipped the power switch and saw the light bulb turn on, I had a flash of insight. A big part of why I'd fallen so far was the way I'd let my thoughts run rampant. The brain does trillions of calculations per second, each one a tiny electrical discharge between synapses, each one a single spark in an intricate chain of patterns and sequences. And each time a synapse fires, it gets stronger, both reducing the resistance and reaction time. Thus, the thought patterns you reinforce are the ones that eventually take control of your mind.

I'd allowed negativity and self-pity to dominate my thoughts. And such thoughts led me to do things that were destructive to my health and wellbeing. As my mother's voice faded away, I resolved to change the way I thought — to replace my negative thoughts with meditations on God as the counselors at Freedom House kept saying I needed to.

And I prayed that I'd desire God in my life more each day, and through that, I'd learn what I needed to in order to have the strength to overcome my own caustic tendencies.

And as if God had heard my prayer, the speaker at our next two-day seminar spoke about authority and submission.

"God never puts someone in a position of authority unless he puts him there for a reason," he lectured. "If you have a problem with your leaders, you need to look for the problem inside yourself instead of placing blame on everyone else. When you're ready for authority, believe me, God will give you some. But until then, you need to develop discipline and humility, or you'll never be able to work with other people. Nobody will follow someone who can't follow others."

His words streaked through me, bringing sparks from my head to my feet. I realized that the problems I was having stemmed not from being shot but from a longstanding stronghold I'd had against accepting authority. I wanted things to happen *my way* — that's why I'd trained so hard in karate, and it was the same reason I'd chased the man who hit my car, ultimately leading to my gunshot wound. All this time, I'd blamed him for shooting me, for ruining my life. But now I saw that unless I learned to submit to authority, I was destined to repeat the same mistakes. So I took a good, hard look at myself, did my best to put my ego aside and prayed, *Lord, help me forgive those people who've wronged me. Help me be the person you want me to be.*

The ensuing months were less a battle of the flesh and more a battle in my mind and spirit. There was no one thing in the program that I couldn't do, but cumulatively, the tremendous discipline it took to stay focused on a daily basis was both energizing and tiring. My energy fluctuated like alternating current, and the only way I managed to push forward was by strictly doing exactly what the mentors told me to do. And I kept remembering what the speaker had said — these people were in authority over me for a reason. And unlike prison, at Freedom House, I had the choice whether to obey or not. I could leave any time I wanted. But as long as I was there, I had the chance to tame my spirit. Also unlike prison, Freedom House invested 30 hours or more of Bible study and spiritual truth into my life each and every week. Truth tested under disciplined learning, which just happens to be the definition of a disciple — a disciplined learner.

JOURNEY TOWARD FREEDOM

The discipline paid off, and several months later, I was awarded the status of a Level 3 — a Student/Mentor.

There were very few Level 3s at that time, meaning that I had plenty of opportunity to mentor the junior students. But with opportunity came responsibility, and I quickly found out that it was important to always set the right example. I remembered what it was like being new to the program. I'd brought a lot of hurt and baggage with me, resulting in my being judgmental about everything, constantly looking for a chink in peoples' armor to point out anything I deemed to be hypocritical. And I saw the same look in most of the new students' eyes.

I knew that the only way to earn their trust was to be the example of what we taught. So I went to work making sure my room was in order and as close to perfect as possible. I studied even harder so I could prove to them that I'd memorized the scriptures. And when I saw one falling away, I took the time to reach out and help him in any way I could.

If someone was having trouble keeping his own bathroom clean, I'd give him the key to mine.

"I can't tell you to do something I'm not doing myself," I'd tell him. "You can check my bathroom anytime. But I expect you to keep yours in the same condition."

And they did come see my bathroom. They checked everything in my room with drill instructor-type scrutiny. In return, I'd inspect their room and help instill whatever discipline I could. Each evening after our classes, I continued to work on the facilities, improving them however I could and doing my best to see that the wiring was all functional and safe.

It was in the middle of a repair job that I suddenly realized something — I'd submitted my spirit to the authority of my mentors. And God had put me in a position of authority, just like the speaker said he would.

That night, before I lay down to rest, I knelt by my bed and gave thanks. I finally had the chance to make a positive impact on other peoples' lives, and although I never dreamed I'd be helping others get free from addiction, I was glad that God saw fit to use me.

It was amazing to actually grasp the thought that I, the broken one, the student, was actually capable of becoming the mentor to someone else. Only God could have done that.

SHORT CIRCUIT

And then, time began to pass more and more quickly. It seemed as though in a flash, the year was over. I became the fourth student to graduate from Freedom House.

But with change comes challenge, mine being that I wasn't sure what to do next. I'd been praying for an answer, but so far, God hadn't supplied me with one. So when Jim approached me and asked what my plans were, I could only shake my head and sigh.

"Actually, I'm not quite sure what I'll be doing," I admitted. "I'm not going back to Alaska, that's for sure. I suppose I might move somewhere new, turn over a new leaf."

"What about working here for a while?" Jim asked. "There is a ton of work to do here around campus, and you would work in well as a facilities manager."

It took me all of two seconds to decide. Even though I'd earned the right to leave with my head held high, it still felt like there was something more I was supposed to accomplish here. Helping with the facilities was the least I could do after all they'd done for me. As a faith-based organization that hangs on by faith and a constant shoestring budget, I realized that God had given me my next step. He'd brought me here not only to graduate the program but to leave it in better shape.

The next day, after my completion ceremony, I set to work getting the facilities up to speed. It took several months of constant work, but by the time I was through, most of the facilities were updated. And in the mean time, I received an offer to go work with Port-A-Pit when my job at Freedom House was over. But I didn't want to leave until I'd trained someone to take my place. My heart had become so connected to the people and what Freedom House stood for. So I set to the task, and a new graduate surfaced at just the right time.

Now I've trained that brother to assume those tasks, and it's finally time for me to move on. I'll never forget my time at Freedom House and will always be thankful for everything they've done for me. So it's with a mixture of joy and nostalgia that I look into the future — joy in the knowledge that my life is upheld by the Lord, nostalgia in the friendships that I'll be distanced from.

Before my life short-circuited completely, I had plenty of things and no friends. But at Freedom House, I had few things and true friends, including the people who invite me to dinner, the ones who drag me along for some relaxation time and the ones who continually check in on me and pray for me. I've finally learned what true friendship is.

Just like when a wire short circuits, sometimes you have to cut your own power off so other people can fix things safely. When I was running on my own energy, I never had enough voltage to make myself change. So, although I know that God is opening up a new chapter in my life, I'll always miss Freedom House and the people who have helped bring out the best in me.

I've heard God referred to as the master carpenter or the true physician. He can build anything, heal anything and work miracles in ways that people can only begin to understand. But in my case, he rewired my life, replaced my fuses and got me running on the right current. So to me, despite my own knuckleheaded ways, I know that God will always be the master electrician, and with his grace and mercy guarding my spiritual fuse box, I'll never short circuit again.

CONCLUSION

How to Have a
Personal Relationship
With Jesus Christ

The transformed lives of the men in *Journey Toward Freedom* all have one thing in common: faith in Jesus Christ that brought the real change and ushered them into an altogether new direction in life. God's love and favor began to restore what their soul's adversary and personal sin had damaged and broken.

You do not have to be a hardcore "dope fiend" or alcoholic to experience such wonderful changes within. The truth is that **all men have sinned and fallen short of the glory of God** (Romans 3:23).

We all stand in need of his saving grace and forgiveness. It is the desire within the very heart of God to turn your personal pain and tragedies into the path to something so much better. He yearns for you to experience his higher purpose for your life. The **Lord has always held a purpose and plan** for you throughout years of failures, destructive habits and wanderings. His Holy Spirit has been drawing you toward this decision to turn around, this point of change that will help launch your own *Journey Toward Freedom* (John 6:44-65).

God's word promises that if we will call upon him sincerely and with all our heart, he will never turn anyone away.

"If you confess with your mouth that Jesus is Lord and believe in your heart that God raised him from the dead, you will be saved. For it is by believing in your heart that you are made right with God, and it is by confessing with your mouth that you are saved." (Romans 10:9-10)*

Ask him: Prayer is simply talking to him as a man talks with his friend. Ask Jesus Christ to forgive you of all the sinful choices and the acts you have committed. Invite him to come and begin his life-changing relationship with you.

CONCLUSION

Believe: Open your own heart up to receive him as Lord and Savior, and you will receive his saving grace.

Trust him: Giving the Lord your heart will also compel you to choose to surrender your own will and ways to walk in his will and ways day by day. As you stay true to this process, you will begin to notice changes inside, changes that will affirm you are learning to walk with your Lord in his new way of living (Psalm 119:11).

Join with other believers: As you study his word (the Holy Bible) and daily and prayerfully look for his guidance, he will lead you to a good Bible-believing church. Locate that church family, one that puts great emphasis and time and effort into teaching the scriptures (Romans 10:17). Your faith will begin to grow, and your walk will get stronger as you mature in spirit.

A *Journey Toward Freedom* always begins with a first step. Please don't put such an important decision off — your new life and purpose will be worth it all.

Eternal life with Christ is the most important gift and decision of all. To accept Jesus is the key to a transformation and to enjoying your new life and future (John 3:1-21).

Let Us Know...

We celebrate with you in this great eternal decision you have made (see Luke 15)! Would you please write to us and let us know if this book has helped you make a positive decision to accept Jesus Christ as the Lord of your life?

If you have taken this step of faith, we encourage you to step out and tell others about your decision and determination to walk with him.

If you need more information to help you in your new walk with the Lord or suggestions of a good church in your area, call, e-mail or write us, and we will do our best to help you.

God bless you greatly as you now experience for yourself this wonderful *Journey Toward Freedom.*

Give Copies of
Journey Toward Freedom
To Others

As you enjoyed reading *Journey Toward Freedom*, perhaps you thought of others who could benefit from this book. Giving them your copy or, better yet, sending them one could possibly jumpstart their own *Journey Toward Freedom* — one that powerfully transforms their lives.

If you would like additional copies for friends or family members, or perhaps your church library, etc., please contact us with your request using the order form on the following page.

Clearly print all the information requested. Presently, a $20.00 minimum should cover our costs, plus shipping and handling. For multiple copies, please call Freedom House Ministries during regular business hours.

Freedom House Ministries (503) 347-9966
Mon-Fri, 10:00 a.m. to 5:00 p.m. PST

Need A Speaker to Bring a
Challenging Message
to Your Church or Organization?

Pastor and Executive Director Jim Cottrell speaks to the issues of involvement with the addicted and the great mission field found within the streets of our own communities. He has a powerful message that motivates and encourages others. With more than 30 years of experience, Jim has been well received as he shares informative and thought provoking messages with various civic organizations and church venues all across denominational lines.

If you are interested in a Freedom House speaker or a team to bring a challenging message to your church or event, or you would like more information on how you or your organization can address addiction issues, please contact us.

If you have family members or loved ones caught up in the heavy consequences of bad choices or destructive habits and they are desperate to change their lives, you can contact us for more information on how to get someone real help through Freedom House.

JOURNEY TOWARD FREEDOM
ORDER FORM

Please Print

Phone: _____

Bill To: _____

Payment Method:

☐ Visa ☐ Master Card ☐ Cash ☐ Check

Card # _____

Exp. Date _____ 3-Digit # on Back _____

Name on Card _____

Card Address _____

City _____ State _____ Zip _____

Signature _____

☐ Order by Phone **SORRY, WE CANNOT ACCEPT COD**

Phone: _____

Ship To: **Please Print**

Quantity	Item	Description	Unit Price	Total
	Book	Journey Toward Freedom	$15.00	
			Shipping	$5.00
			Misc.	
			Donation	
			Balance Due	

Freedom House Ministries

P.O. Box 33150

Portland, OR 97292-3150

Phone: (503) 347-9966

Fax: (503) 542-0459

A 501 (c) 3 Non-Profit Ministry

CONCLUSION

Would You Like to
Partner
With Freedom House?

Addiction is destroying the lives of multitudes, and nearly every home has experienced tragedy or suffered loss due to drug or alcohol abuse in their immediate or extended family. The overwhelming number of addicts represents one of the biggest mission fields and God-given opportunities of our time.

There are great mission fields overseas, but do not overlook the challenge of the great mission field right here in our own urban and rural communities.

Almost every person who interviews and commits to Freedom House comes here extremely broken and has little or no financial wherewithal to offer to help toward the daily expenses of their bed space, utilities, meals and, most importantly, the Christian training and mentoring each one receives over the course of an entire year.

Have the true stories of men like Bill, Isaac, Nick, Phil, Ryan, Derick or Pat stirred your heart? Perhaps you'd like to partner with us in helping to rescue other men who are lost, drunken or dope sick. Freedom House staff members answer phone calls for help daily. Truly the harvest is ripe, and the laborers are still so very few! Are you called to this type of work? One way to know is to step out and **volunteer your time.**

Perhaps you would like to help **share the financial burden.** We welcome the opportunity for your faith to join ours. You can make a significant difference in the lives of the addicted as a sponsoring partner. With your financial gifts, you help us meet basic needs — such as warm beds and nutritious meals.

Or, you can help keep our doors open and operating with your **regular monthly gifts.** Your caring support will enable us to continue to provide hope, training and Christian love on an ongoing basis. And, above all, your gifts of time and finances help us meet spiritual needs. We teach God's word in a Christ-centered, warm and loving way. We also provide a structured and highly accountable and disciplined environment.

Freedom House Ministries is a registered not-for-profit organization. We are an independent work, so your generous support is tax deductible and so greatly appreciated.

Honor Loved Ones
With a Memorial Gift to
Freedom House

Every so often, families have reflected on the work of Freedom House as a fitting way to honor their loved ones who have passed on through Memorial Gifts. Others have chosen to do the same as they honor someone living and beloved in a special way. These gifts will do so much good here to help men find their own *Journey Toward Freedom.* Contact us for more information.

Your Gifts
Make a Huge Difference!

Freedom House Ministries is a faith-based, independent organization. As a registered 501(c)3 not-for-profit charity, Freedom House Ministries receives neither state nor federal funding to operate daily. Our operations are supported predominantly by grassroots, caring and committed individuals, businesses and church families.

Our staff members and their families are called to this type of work and have operated in faith, believing in God for his help and daily provision with some having served in this capacity for more than two decades.

With a faith-based approach, we have chosen to never turn anyone away for lack of funds, trusting the Lord who knows the need. We believe he will touch the hearts of caring people, churches and businesses to step forward and help underwrite these life-changing efforts in their own special and unique ways. We appreciate your prayers and support as the addicted are a huge part of our population.

CONCLUSION

We'd Love to Have You Visit Us...

Freedom House Ministries holds daily chapel times that are open to the public, and we would be happy to provide you with more information or a tour. If you are in the Portland, Oregon, area and would like to attend any of our sessions, please contact our office.

How to contact
Freedom House Ministries

Mailing Address:
Freedom House Ministries
PO Box 33150
Portland, OR 97292-3150

Campus Address:
Freedom House
8613 NE St Johns Road
Vancouver, WA 98665

(503) 347-9966
Mon-Fri, 10:00 a.m. to 5:00 p.m. PST

Web site: FreedomHouseMinistries.net

Email: Info@FreedomHouseMinistries.net

For more information on reaching your city with stories from your church, please contact Good Catch Publishing at www.goodcatchpublishing.com

GOOD CATCH
PUBLISHING

Did one of these stories touch you?
Did one of these real people move you to tears?
Tell us (and them) about it on our reader blog at
www.goodcatchpublishing.blogspot.com.